Trine,

Man Up,

Already!

Love you more than
You Know! Thank
You for your love
and support!

— John —

Man Up, Already!

How to Live and Lead at Home and in the Marketplace

John C. Puritz

FOREWORD

"Man Up, Already! is a book that is long overdue. Be prepared to be called out, challenged, and inspired! John is raising the bar for men, and the women who love them, and he is transparently sharing his personal journey along the way. John's style is fun, engaging, and direct, with a sense of humility and passion. Hold on tight! You are in for a fun ride!" - Alejandra Veder, book coach and author of "Unleash the Woman Within".

ABOUT THE AUTHOR

John C. Puritz is on a mission, and he's calling out men in the 21st century to stand up and lead. With over 25 years of teaching, mentoring, and coaching experience, John wants to educate, equip, and empower today's man to "Man Up" and learn how to become the amazing man God created him to be! Drawing from both the Old and New Testaments, and from personal experiences, John provides a fresh perspective on how to live and lead in today's world.

Whether you are a husband, father, or a young man just beginning your journey, here you will find an engaging book on how to tap into what already exists and learn how to play full out in your life. For wives and mothers, John helps to shed some light on what society is trying to take away from the men you love so much. "Man Up, Already!" will inspire you to powerfully move forward in your life.

John lives in South Florida with his wife Tricia, and their two children, Sofia and Ethan.

NOTE TO THE READER

The original title of this book was "Man the F Up!" but was changed because the "F" in the title could have been misconstrued as something else. "Man Up, Already!" conveyed the message just as well!

As men, we are called to lead our family, finances, and firm (business life) with faith. To be the men God called us to be, we need to lead with integrity, humility, authenticity, and morality. I call these the "Four Pillars."

My goal with this book is to help men realize that we are created by God to be far more than society has led us to believe. Something is wrong with men today. Something is missing. I've spent the better part of twenty-three years learning, leading, mentoring, and coaching men and women, and both are unfulfilled. Men know something is wrong within their spirit, and many women are wondering what happened to the men they dreamt of to partner with in life and lead the way through an amazing journey together.

Drawing from Biblical characters and my own personal experiences, I hope to provoke, touch, move, and inspire men to see beyond societal norms and strive to become something greater. After all, we are more "human becomings" than we are human beings.

I, in no way shape or form, intend to convey that I am somehow beyond what I'm discussing. We live in a very real world, and we all struggle with some very real things on a daily basis. I'm writing from a space of authenticity and transparency. The first three chapters of the book will focus on my personal journey in order to provide you, the reader, with context for the content that follows. I'm on a journey to constantly improve, and want to inspire others to do the same. I hope this book helps you find what you've been looking for, or at least gets you moving in the right direction.

ACKNOWLEDGEMENTS

My sincere gratitude goes to six incredibly influential men in my life, without whom this journey simply wouldn't have been possible.

Marc S. Puritz: for instilling in me integrity, honor, character, and grit.

Pastor Rich Joy: for being the mentor and guide I needed as a young husband and father, and for setting me on the path.

John Eldredge: for writing *Wild at Heart* and drawing out the warrior within.

Steven J. Leatherman: for being a true "Brother in Arms" and accepting me for who I am, and not being afraid to hold me accountable. You have what it takes!

Pastor Tim Williams: for being a true brother, pastor, and friend. What an incredible journey we've been on so far!

Mark Marchesani: for being the man of God that you are and demonstrating for me what it looks like to step out into the bigger picture.

To my book coach Alejandra Veder: Thank you for being an incredible coach, with an incredible system. You lighted the path and enabled the entire process to happen. It simply couldn't have happened without you!

To Tricia, Sofia, and Ethan...

Thank you for giving me a reason to fight every day.

CONTENTS

INTRODUCTION

It's a lie.

"Go to school." "Get good grades." "Get a good job." It's all a lie. And the crazy thing is everyone believes it.

You see, I followed that plan, and I followed it to the letter. I worked really hard—for five years, in fact—to finally get my Bachelors of Music from Manhattanville College in Harrison, New York. I then began a teaching career in music and worked my way up from private elementary school, teaching socially and emotionally disturbed children, to public middle school and high school. All the while, I was working hard to get my Master's Degree in Teaching from Sacred Heart University in Fairfield Connecticut. In fact, I received high honors on both degrees.

Get good grades? Check! Get a good job? Check!

In 1999, I got the "dream job." I was running a high school instrumental music program in

Stamford, Connecticut. My wife Tricia and I bought a house, had our daughter Sofia, and worked *really* hard. Tricia worked, Sofia went to day care, and I spent twelve to fifteen hours a day, six days a week, building a music program with the focus on "someday."

In 2002, I received my Master's degree and "someday" arrived. You know what that day is, right? It's the day you can financially breathe again, the day you can start living better. And we did. We ate out. We started working on the house. We got connected to a great church. Then, we had Ethan. We were overjoyed. But two months later, he went into day care, and it threw us back five years financially. It was time to climb up the down escalator all over again.

We did everything we were told to do according to the plan... but it didn't work. So we left it. We sold our house, packed everything up, and moved to Florida.

We found out that the successful, wealthy, upper class thought differently, acted differently, and lived differently, and we wanted the same thing. Fifteen years later, with many ups and downs and twists and turns, we have learned that it's all an inside job. It's all in our head.

Do you want a great life? It's out there waiting for you to take it.

Do you want prosperity? It's one emotional goal away. Do you want health & wellness? One decision backed by discipline can bring everything you want right to you!

I want to help you learn to be your best self first, so that you can do all the things your best self does and have all the things your best self has.

Will it be hard? Yes! Will it be life-changing? You bet! Will it be worth it? If you follow my guidance, you will learn to live a life that is more passionate, beautiful, and full than you can possibly imagine. Let's go!

CHAPTER 1

BEGINNINGS AND BACKGROUND

I'd love to tell you that I had a normal, functional, happy childhood, but really, who does? And what is "normal," anyway?

My parents married young, as so many did in the '60s and '70s. There were many happy moments, and I have incredible parents, but their marriage unfortunately ended when I was very young.

My sister and I lived with my mother, who worked her tail off to take care of us, and we saw my father every other weekend. My mom had an incredibly challenging task in front of her in raising two children, and there are no words I could write here to describe my respect for her, as well as for all single moms. What they do to provide for their children is mind-blowing. The respect I have for my mom today, thinking back on all she had to do, is without measure. She did her best. She gave her all to take care of us. Our life wasn't perfect, and many times it simply sucked. But she never quit!

My mother eventually remarried a man who had two children as well. There were a lot of issues in our home at that time, which made life extremely challenging.

My father lived about two hours away. To see us, he would drive two hours back and forth on Friday and Sunday every other week. My sister and I spent a lot of time in the car. I often think about my father, who was in his twenties and thirties during those times, and what kind of sacrifices he made to see his kids. I watched my mom struggle every day, but I wasn't able to see how my dad did. What was his day to day process like?

Needless to say, we played a lot of games, had great conversations, and listened to a lot of music to pass the time. Because he would only come every other weekend, my father became almost mythical to us. He was our hero, as so many dads are to their kids.

It's funny to look back on those times now.

Here was this twenty-something year old guy, trying to entertain two small children. Everything seemed like an incredible adventure to us.

I'll give you an example: in 1975, when the movie *Jaws* came out, my dad wanted to go see it very badly. Of course, having two elementary school-aged children wasn't going to stand in his way! He was a man who was going to get what he wanted. So he took us to that movie, and the nightmares that followed are the stuff of legend. Today, I'm still afraid to go into the ocean for fear of sharks. I have a love/hate relationship with them; I'm totally intrigued by sharks, and yet scared out of my mind. There were so many other moments like that— moments of adventure, emotional trauma, and emotional craziness. Growing up as a divorced child was an incredibly unique and tough experience, and realizing how much I didn't want my children to have to ever experience that became imprinted on me.

When I was fourteen years old, my father came to me and said, "I really want you to come live with me." I can still remember that moment and how powerful it was. I wanted to be with my father. I wanted to be close to him. A boy needs his father. It is inescapable. I needed him. I wanted to be around him. I wanted him to lead me and guide me, and I jumped at the opportunity. The challenge was that I had to go tell my mom.

This would have been a tough task under normal circumstances, but my mom was also going through some serious personal trauma during this time. You see, my mother had just lost her mother, and they had a very strong bond. She had essentially just lost her hero, and now I was going to have to tell her that I was leaving as well. That was very challenging for a fourteen-year-old to process and have the courage to do. I can still remember the gut-wrenching emotion of knowing there was no easy way to break my mom's heart.

I caused my mom an immense amount of pain, but I knew that if I did not take my father's offer, I would die inside. I truly believe today that if I had stayed where I was, I would have either been incarcerated or on drugs. Back then, I was such a broken, insecure follower with such little hope for the future, I know I would have followed the negative influence. With no strong male figure to guide me, I would have drifted. Today, we place that burden on single mothers, but they cannot be two parents. They are mothers, not fathers. One person cannot fill two roles, especially with boys. Boys need men to guide them.

Think about how important dads are to their children, especially in their early teen years. We as dads foster them and mentor them. We are their hope. We are their guide. We are so much of what they need at that specific time in their lives.

So I did it; I moved in with my dad at fourteen years of age.

My father had a unique way of parenting.

His idea of good parenting was: "Okay. Here's the rope. Don't hang yourself with it, because if you do, it's not going to be good."

Now, that was a drastically different way of parenting than my mom's, and it took a while to adapt to it. What evolved, though, was a huge amount of respect. I didn't want to disrespect my dad. I understood that he was bestowing something on me, some place of honor: "Hey, I love you and I trust you. You're man enough to handle this." It was like being knighted.

During that time, my father also remarried, so my dad, his new wife, and I all constructed a new life together.

We had to sort out the boundaries, the rules, and the freedoms. We were finding it all out together, and it was a very exciting time. It was a new life—a rebirth. I had to figure out what kind of man I was going to be.

PASSION

Music is and always was a huge part of my life. I started playing drums in elementary school and took to them very quickly. Playing the drums was something I knew I could be good at. It just fit me. They became an escape. Drumming became an identity for me. I wasn't really good at sports, but I was really good at drumming, and I poured my heart and soul into it.

Because I was so broken and insecure as a kid, drumming also became a barrier, a hiding place. It became something that enabled me to not have to deal with my brokenness. I could put on a totally different persona and be a different person. I could be a new creation, another man, and I saw that as total freedom. I embraced my ability to use drums to hide.

I didn't know this at the time, but my "drummer persona" was an imposter, or a "false self." My entire identity was wrapped up into being a drummer. Once, my sister and I were talking, and I said, "You know, if people just knew that I played the drums, they would like me." I remember that moment very specifically. I think about that young man now, and how sad he really was. In today's society, how many young men are searching for an identity with no sense of self and no sense of worth? The answer is quite a few!

Without going on a major tangent here, look at school violence in our country today. What's happening with our young men? Social media has amplified this lack of identity. Finding out who you are and your place in the world during the teen years is hard enough, but now, with the prevalence of social media, we are trading authenticity for fallacy. No one really knows who anyone else is. Combine that with low self-esteem, little to no strong relationships, and lack of male leadership, and we have a recipe for disaster. I'm not trying to solve our societal problems here, nor get into a gun violence debate. All I'm saying is that we need to really pay attention to our young men by talking to them and with them. We need to let them know we are listening, and not encourage them to keep it all inside, where it can fester and grow.

I constructed this musical personality

throughout high school, and people started to know me as "the drummer." I started playing in bands at fifteen years old with the dream of one day becoming a rock star.

I was a mediocre student at best during my first years of high school. The truth is, I was lazy—plain and simple. I also developed a real sense of entitlement. I felt like I was owed something, that I *deserved* something, and I carried that point of view with me for a very long time.

Thankfully, something happened to me during my junior year of high school. Something inside me said, "You know what? You need to get your act together. You really need to knock it off and get serious."

So, I kicked it in gear. I got accepted into a Liberal Arts program at the University of Hartford, with the idea of moving into their Hartt School of Music. During my freshman year, I took routine general classes, patiently waiting for my opportunity to audition.

What I've neglected to mention is that I had no real formal drum training up until this point.

I had pretty much taught myself. It wasn't until my senior year of high school that I even took on a teacher. So there I was, totally oblivious and totally entitled, with the opportunity to audition for one of the top music schools in the Northeast. Needless to say, it didn't go very well. In fact, the woman in charge of the audition who sat behind what I referred to as the "Table of Doom" looked at me and said, "Maybe you ought to consider doing something different with your life."

You know that happy ending in the '80s movie "Flashdance," where the main character dances her butt off and gets accepted into the school of her dreams? Yeah, that didn't happen!

I vividly remember that moment. It was the first time I had to really question what I wanted in my life. I asked myself, "Is she right? Or am I going to do something about it and stick to this?" I wasn't ready to quit, so I transferred into the University of Bridgeport and got accepted into their music program.

There is a huge point to this: we spend so much time moaning and complaining about what doesn't turn out right, we never realize that God has much bigger plans. If I hadn't gotten turned down by the Hartt School of Music, I wouldn't be writing this book. I never would have gone down the path He had for me. Part of "manning up" is taking the hits life gives you, then finding a way to keep going. Life is for sure going to knock you on your butt. It's unavoidable. It's how we respond to the hit that matters!

There's a great scene in the movie "Rocky Balboa" that illustrates this. Rocky's son is also displaying entitlement issues, and criticizes his father for chasing his dream. Rocky finally pauses and teaches his son a valuable lesson. He says:

"Let me tell you something you already know. The world ain't all sunshine and rainbows. It's a very mean and nasty place, and I don't care how tough you are, it will beat you to your knees, and keep you there permanently, if you let it. You, me, or nobody is gonna hit as hard as life. But it ain't about how hard you hit. It's about how hard you can get hit, and keep moving forward. How much you can take, and keep moving forward. That's how winning is done!"

So get your butt up and keep going! How important are your goals? Are you willing to deal with the hard and nasty stuff, or are you going to fold like a cheap lawn chair?

I spent three years at the University of Bridgeport getting my music education degree. During that time, I would go to school during the day, play music at night, work during the day on the weekends, and gig Friday and Saturday nights. I did that all the way through college.

At twenty years old, I hooked up with a band called "Beijing Blast" and played with them till I was twenty-six years old. We did so many incredible things; things I could only dream about when I was a kid. We got on a small record label and eventually played with some big name acts. A lot of the things I imagined while air-drumming as a kid in my bedroom came true, just on a very small level. We recorded, played great venues, were well known in the area, and were even on the radio. I remember driving down US 1 in Norwalk, Connecticut one summer night, listening to our song on the radio. What a thrill! It was a great run. And for some, that's good enough. But for me, something changed. I can't really tell you when it changed, or how, but something did change. And it changed in a way that redefined me as a young man trying to figure it all out.

CHAPTER 2

HERITAGE, RELIGION, AND RELATIONSHIP

I grew up Jewish. My mother and father came from Jewish households, but our Judaism mostly extended to performing the rituals, celebrating the holidays, and honoring our heritage. At thirteen years old, I was a Bar Mitzvah.

For me, Judaism was more about heritage than religious belief. I had very little connection with or relationship to God, and over time, I looked at being Jewish as nothing more than an identity. To me, it had very little meaning beyond that. I definitely had no strong *relationship* with God.

When I moved into my father's house and he got remarried, his wife was a Baptist, and she was a big believer in Jesus Christ. To make things even more interesting, I was attending a Roman Catholic private high school. I went there because my dad believed it was the best education you could get as a high school student in that area during that time.

I'll never forget the first day we had to go to mandatory mass. It was the first time I had been exposed to a true Roman Catholic service. There I was in the middle of a gymnasium, with the entire student body responding together at the appropriate times, and I had no idea what was going on! I thought I had missed some secret meeting or something. I can look back on it now and laugh, but at the time, it was bizarre.

When I was around fourteen or fifteen years old, I began to notice some very mixed messages coming at me in terms of spirituality and religion. I knew I was Jewish, and I honored that very deeply. I truly did believe there was a God, and I couldn't believe that all of life was just an accident. At the same time, I had no real relationship with Him, nor was I seeking one. I just knew He was there.

I never could buy into the idea that everything was just random or that God didn't exist; but the concept of having a relationship with my creator was also very foreign. In my experience, everything that pertained to God was filtered through religion. You had to "do this" or "do that" to receive blessing and favor, and I rebelled against that idea. Having to do something to gain favor didn't make any sense to me. How could one speak of unconditional love, yet have to earn it? It didn't equate. So, I tuned it out and escaped into music and the crazy world of the late '80s/early '90s hard rock scene.

That went on for quite a time, until the winter of 1994. I was twenty-four years old and on a ski trip with a friend of mine in the Catskill Mountains of New York. We ended up getting his pick-up truck stuck in a river in the middle of nowhere, in an area that had gotten hit with some very severe snow and ice storms. While my buddy was tasked with trying to get the truck out of the river, my job was to carry the supplies from the truck to the cabin, about a quarter of a mile away, in waist-deep snow.

During one of my trips back to the truck, God very clearly told me to lie down in the snow. What happened next transformed my life. He told me to look up, and I saw Him. That was very clear. He revealed Himself to me, not as a man, but in everything around me. The prophet Ezekiel describes an experience very similar to this in Ezekiel 43:2 (NKJV):

"And behold, the glory of the God of Israel came from the way of the east. His voice was like the sound of many waters; and the earth shone with His glory."

It was in that moment, in the mountains of New York, that I knew He was real and He loved me. There was such clarity and certainty in that moment, it completely shook me.

I was never the same after that encounter, and it led me to start asking questions and seeking some real truths.

The Bible says that after God tells Jesus, "This is my Son, whom I love; with him I am well pleased" (Matthew 3:17 NIV), He sends him out to the desert to be tested. Well, I think God decided that I needed some testing of my own!

THE DESERT YEAR

Shortly after the experience in the mountains, I

found myself stripped of all that I thought was important to me. My three-year relationship with my girlfriend ended. My best friend felt it was time to move his girlfriend into our apartment, and time for me to move out. And so, for the first time in my life, I was living alone in a very small studio apartment with no one to talk to but myself. I was the most depressed I had ever been in my entire life.

I'm sharing this story with you so you can get a picture of the man I was before God got a serious hold of me. I was a drummer in a hard rock band by night and a public school teacher by day. It was like I had a split personality, and I was very much in conflict. To be completely transparent, I was a total poser. As a matter of fact, I didn't even go by the name John when I played in the band. I went by a nickname. I would be out in this crazy music world playing one person, then show up daily in another reality as Mr. Puritz the music teacher. I was lost, and I was dying inside. I was depressed and seeking validation from anyone who'd give it to me. I had no idea who I was, and was seeking the person who could tell me who that might be. In fact, if it weren't for the fact that there were children in a classroom waiting for me to show up and impact them, I would have been perfectly okay with my life ending at that point.

I look back on that young man in his mid-twenties with such sadness. He was so lost! Maybe you can relate to my circumstances; I was so broken inside that I preferred to spend time with others more broken than me rather than deal with my own garbage and junk. It wasn't until I hit a breaking point in early 1996, at twenty-six years old, that God started to lead me out of the wilderness.

REDEMPTION

As a gift, my stepmother gave me *The Message*, which was a version of the New Testament of the Bible written in modern day language. As I read Jesus's words in plain English, something wonderful happened inside me. I realized that his message wasn't about religion, but about having a strong, personal relationship with God, the Creator of the Universe. It was about a standard, and about dedicating my life to something far greater than myself. It was bigger than me and my circumstances.

I needed something to grab onto during that time. I needed something firm and solid to hold while everything else around me was shifting. I needed to grab on to something that I believed could define my life, and when I read his words—when I read how much God loved me and how he sent his son to die for me—something inside me said, "I can buy into this; I can hold onto this; this needs to be the measuring line for my life moving forward."

I remember standing there in that moment, wondering, "If I do this, am I no longer a Jew?" I understood that maybe the Jewish community would say I wasn't, and maybe the Christian community would say so as well, but in my heart, I knew my newfound relationship with God made me a more powerful Jew. To this day, I stand by that conviction.

I am so proud of who I am as a Jew, and also who I am in Christ. It is something that has defined my life. I gave my heart to Christ, and I have been in a relationship with him for the last twenty-three years. It has been an absolutely incredible, amazing relationship.

Regardless of your feelings about my

spirituality and beliefs, know that you are entitled to them. I'm only sharing my story, and explaining how all of this has shaped the man I am. I'm sure both sides—Jewish and Christian—will have their own opinions.

CHAPTER 3

MARRIAGE AND THE ADVENTURE

At the time of writing this book, my wife Tricia and I have been married for twenty-one years. We met each other in college, when I was nineteen and she was eighteen, and I'd love to tell you that we were college sweethearts and all of that romantic stuff, but that's just not the way it happened.

We met at a party right before the term officially started, and she didn't think twice about me. If you asked her what her thoughts were regarding me in that moment, she'd say, "What a freak!" But for me, when I saw her, the world stopped. It was lust at first sight. I can still see her in my mind. She literally took my breath away.

As fate would have it, during the second semester of that year, we ended up having a class together, and we struck up a friendship.

That winter, I got back together with my high school girlfriend, so Trish and I just became very good friends. And because I was commuting to college, I would stay in her room between classes to sleep off whatever late-night gigs I had while she was out. Unfortunately, Trish then transferred away to another college, and we only corresponded through letters and occasional phone calls.

The friendship Trish and I built during those years became very strong. In fact, I considered her one of my best friends, and would set her up with other friends of mine. Meanwhile, I was in other chaotic relationships. But she was always there.

It's so easy to look back and see God's plan—His hand working in our lives. But when we are going through hard moments, we tend not to see the bigger picture.

About five years later, during the "Desert Year," Trish came out for my birthday to see me and the band play. Her side of the story is that when she pulled into my driveway, she knew instantly that I was the man she wanted to marry. I, on the other hand, looked at her and thought, *There's my good friend.* I didn't even think twice about her except to note that she still looked really good. Well, very long story short: we ended up kissing that night and were both blindsided by it.

When friends move into a romantic relationship, it can be very tricky to navigate, especially when one person is as broken as I was. We ended up dating for a few months, but I wasn't ready at all for what she brought to the table. I was screwed up in the head and didn't want to lose my best friend, and I knew that if we kept going, I was going to crush her. I had to man up! I had to take a moment, regroup, and learn how to take a stand (I'll talk about this later on in the book). I had to bolster my integrity and find my character. All of this was right before my stepmother gave me *The Message.*

So, we broke up. We stopped seeing each other. We talked very infrequently for a good six months. I was drinking. I was dating. I was sleeping around. I was doing all the things that you do to hide from your issues, and hurting a lot of people throughout the process. For that, I am very sorry. That's when God really got a hold of me.

At a breaking point, I remember lying in bed and looking up at the ceiling, analyzing my life, completely unhappy and exhausted. I literally called out, "Okay, God, what do you want?" I was done fighting. I had completely given myself up to Him. Can you relate? Maybe you've been in that scenario: when you've given it everything you have and it's not working. At this point, there's nothing left to do but admit defeat.

I said, "What do you want?" and Tricia popped into my head and wouldn't come out. In that moment, I picked up the phone and said, "Listen, I want you to know that I love you and I want to spend my life with you. You're probably with someone else and I've missed my opportunity, but I just needed to say that so I can move on."

We've been together ever since.

Our relationship was never perfect. We continue to grow and get better, and she's a woman who fights. She stands by me through it all, the good and the bad. Again, it's never perfect, and from the outside, it may look easy. But it never is. Marriage takes work. It has its ups and downs. And when you put it all together, it's one heck of an adventure.

In the book *Wild at Heart,* John Eldredge says that a man has to have a "beauty to rescue." Tricia, for sure, is mine.

THE ADVENTURE

Trish and I got married at twenty-seven and twenty-six years old, and we did what everybody tells you you're supposed to do. We went right inside "the box" that everybody tells you you're supposed to be in: go to school, get good grades, get a good job, get married, buy a house, have kids. We did it all. And we did it by the book!

At thirty-three years old, I was working probably twelve to fifteen hours a day running a high school music program forty-five minutes from our house. Trish also was working, and our two children, Sofia and Ethan, were in daycare. We were grinding it out!

Maybe you, the reader, are that kind of guy

too. I mean, that's most men, right? We're workers and providers, doing all the things that we're supposed to do. We're husbands, fathers, sons, brothers, and church men; you name it, we're grinding. We're showing up in our lives day by day, doing the same thing over and over, wondering if this is really all there is.

Financially, we were surviving, but we weren't getting ahead. We felt like the vehicle of our lives was spinning its tires in the mud.

During this time, I went to my pastor and said, "You know, life doesn't feel so good, yet everybody says we have a great life." He said to me, "You know, John, you ought to read this book," and he handed me *Wild at Heart* by John Eldredge. I'm going to reference that book throughout this one quite often because it's an amazing book that has had a profound effect on my life. I wouldn't be the man I am without John's book. I read that book and realized that I had created an entire life based on fear.

Obviously, there's a story there.

When I was in college, music majors had to pick which direction they were going to focus their studies in: performance or music education. They didn't have all the other programs that exist today. I went to my drum instructor at the time and said, "Hey, what should I do?" He said, "Pick education, so you don't sleep in your car as a starving musician. You'll always have a job." That conversation had a huge impact on the course of my life. He could have said, "Listen, do you believe in yourself? Do you believe you've got talent? Well, if you do, don't let anybody put you in a box. Get out there, make your way in the world, and fight for what you want!" He could have said that, but he didn't. Why? Because he was a teacher. What he said was "get a teaching degree so you don't sleep in your car," and in that moment, I created my reality. I simply believed that if I didn't have a good job, I would sleep in my car and be a starving musician. The comment didn't really have anything to do with him; it's just how I processed what he said.

So I went down the education route, and that decision, born out of fear, created a life on a teacher's income. When I read *Wild at Heart,* I knew that God had bigger plans for me. I looked at the decisions I had made, found they were all based on fear, and said, "God, I've not let you lead. I've never given myself to you."

Trish and I decided we were going to give everything up, sell our house, and resign our jobs. We would take our kids, who were five years old and eight months old at the time, and move to Florida to start all over. We wanted to move to Florida because... well, it's Florida! And when you're from the Northeast... well, it's Florida!

We had three goals when we moved:

1. Keep Trish home.

2. Keep our children out of daycare.

3. Make a six-figure income so we could make the life we wanted possible.

Nobody would hire me. After all, my resume said teacher, but I was ready for the next step! I knew I had skills, talents, and abilities. I had spent ten years building and running music programs, and it was time for the next level. I was looking for somebody to give me a shot, and I knew that if I worked my tail off, I could do it.

One of the main points Eldredge makes in *Wild at Heart* is that most men are asking the question, "Do I have what it takes?"

I knew I did, and through the grace of God and some incredible circumstances, we started a business and began working very hard. For almost fifteen years now, we've been successful entrepreneurs.

There's so many lessons to learn from that process. To sum them up, you've got to have *character* and *conviction*. You have to believe in yourself! You've got to realize that nobody really cares what your issues are. They don't care about what you're dealing with, because they're too busy dealing with whatever *they're* dealing with. That's all they care about!

We spend a lot of time worrying about what people think and care about, but the truth is: they don't! They're too preoccupied with thinking about whatever *they're* thinking about.

When you learn that lesson, you really are free to go create and do incredible, amazing things; and that's why I wrote this book. I want to help men get back to who they were created to be. When we stop drifting and stop doing all the stupid stuff we do to numb ourselves and become desensitized, when we get back to the essence of who God created us to be, it's monumental and magical! Incredible things happen, and the world needs incredible men today. You'll see why in the next chapter.

CHAPTER 4

MODERN MEN AND THE DESIRES OF WOMEN

I wanted to write this book for two main reasons: first, to shed some light on what is happening with men today in our country. If you are unfamiliar with the statistics, it's alarming! We really have drifted off-course.

DIVORCE

Fifty percent of all marriages in the U.S. will end in divorce. Fifty percent!

Picture this: a man and a woman stand at an altar, gazebo, or beach, hold hands, and say, "I will be with you till death do us part," and yet fifty percent of those marriages will end in divorce!

SINGLE PARENTS

Twenty-six percent of children in the U.S. are in single-parent homes. Let your mind really grasp that for a moment: twenty-six percent of kids are going to grow up without the influence of both a father and a mother. Can you take a guess as to which parent is more likely to have the greater influence?

PORNOGRAPHY

200,000 Americans are classified as porn addicts, and over 40 million Americans regularly visit pornography sites. Thirty-five percent of downloads on the Internet today are related to pornography. Two-thirds of porn users are men.

ADDICTION

The National Institute on Drug Abuse says, "Men are more likely than women to use almost all types of illicit drugs, relating in more emergency room visits and deaths from overdose than women."

GUN VIOLENCE

Eighty-six percent of gun deaths result from men.

Gentlemen, we are losing, plain and simple. I want to paint a picture for you: fifty percent of us are going to get a divorce, while twenty-six percent of our children will not live with us. We're most likely to become addicted to pornography, and we will do more drugs and commit more gun violence than women. This is not what God intended when he created men. We have to, and can, do better.

Read those statistics again, and imagine that you knew your son (whether you have one right now or not) was going to end up as a man like that. Wouldn't you want to do something about it to keep it from happening? Of course you would, and that's why we need to start seriously talking about what's happening with men today. None of us would want that for our children, but it's likely to happen if we continue to keep these issues packed away in the closet.

Though this book can and will appeal to a wide variety of people, its focus is towards the "millennial man," because that's the generation that needs to hear this the most. In case you didn't know this already, the millennial generation is the largest generation our country has ever seen. Their impact on our nation and our world will be massive, yet we've done a great job of teaching them that just showing up is trophy-worthy. We've done a very good job of letting them off the hook and keeping them from learning through pain and adversity. We've done an amazing job of helping them avoid the very things that build character and conviction. In order to have a testimony, there has to be a test, and we've spent entirely too much time denying them theirs. We told them, "Go to school, get good grades, and you'll get a job. Follow that path, and you'll be successful." Most of them are graduating from institutions that have charged them a significant amount of money, yet there are fewer jobs in their degree field and/or their income is significantly less than the debt they took on in student loans to get the degree that promised them their success. That's a heck of a lesson we've given them.

WHAT WOMEN WANT

The second reason I made the decision to write this book was to bring to light what women really want from men. I have been teaching, mentoring, and coaching for about twenty-three years now, and there's always a running theme with women when they talk about what they want from a man.

I had a great opportunity to speak with one of my good friends recently, and when I asked her, "What is it that you want from a man?" she listed these qualities: "I want him to listen, share, be a leader, make decisions, protect and be protective, be supportive, be sensitive, be a good lover, have his own identity, be a provider and a great father, give me quality time and yet have his own goals, understand who he is, and have his own friends and his own life so that we're not always on top of each other."

When I took a "30,000-foot view" of that list, I saw that if you boil all of those qualities down and sum them up, women are seeking three things: they need us to be a leader, they need us to be confident, and they need us to be a creator.

Let me clarify.

LEADER

Leaders lead. Leaders are decisive, protective, and supportive. Leaders make decisions. Look at men today. Are we leading? The proof often says something to the contrary. I can't tell you how many times I've interviewed, mentored, and coached a married man who wants to move himself into action to better his family and life. He needs help taking the steps forward (as we all do!), and yet the answer I get most often is "I've got to get permission from my wife."

Guys, a woman doesn't want to give permission, she wants to have things *discussed*. There's a big difference between permission and discussion.

Most men, because of who they are on the inside and what they struggle with, think it's easier to get permission. But here's what's really happening: when we ask a woman for permission, what we're hoping for is that she'll say no, because then we're off the hook! We're not obligated. We then don't have to lead or be decisive. We don't have to take any risks, because we abdicate our authority. We have passed it on to our wives, and we get to cop out. That's not what a woman wants, and deep down inside, that's not what we want either. Deep down inside lies the passion that God has placed inside us all. We've just been trapped inside a lie for so long that we've lost our way and we don't know how to fight back. Sadly, most men don't even think they'll win the battle.

A woman wants to be involved; she wants to share. She wants to have a discussion, and in healthy households, you'll often find women saying, "Well, in the end, if you believe this is what's right for our family, you're the leader of our household." Why? Because they want us to lead.

Back in 2009, our family was greatly impacted by the Recession, and everything we had built in Florida up to that point was in jeopardy. We had built a successful business that was just about to go to the next level, but all of it fell apart and we found ourselves living in my in-laws' house. Needless to say, we felt dejected, overwhelmed, and scared. It was a very difficult time for us. When you are at your lowest, things can look very dark and very scary. Those are also the times when you really learn what you are made of and how strong your relationships are.

One night, I looked at Trish and asked, "What if we left the business?" What I was looking for was a cop-out. I was looking for her to take the lead and let me off the hook. I wanted her to take a position of strength and tell me what to do next. Her response was a life-altering moment that brought about significant change. Trish said, "If that is what you think is best, you are the leader of our family, and we will follow your decision." That was when I really understood that she was in this with me forever, and that even though it was a scary, stressful time, she wanted me to lead. I couldn't escape it, but I could change it. Trish wasn't married to our business or our success. She was married to me, the man I currently was, and the man she believed I could be. Again, it was a life-changing moment for me, and I've truly led our family ever since. We work together and respect each other's strengths and weaknesses. As I've stated earlier, it's never perfect. We have our ups and downs and our fair share of screw-ups, but we work through them together.

CONFIDENCE

Women want men who are secure in themselves. They want to know that we feel secure, that we're comfortable with ourselves, and that we're confident in what's going on around us. Confidence is being secure in one's self. And when a man is confident, he has goals (we're going to spend some time in this book on goals and why they're important). He knows what he wants, and he knows how to get it. That's confidence, and it's very attractive.

Women want us to be good lovers. Well, what makes a man a good lover? Confidence. Now, don't get me wrong—men want pleasure, and a lot of it! But at the same time, confident men also want to give. When I'm intimate with my wife, I want to please her. I'm not in it just for me. I want to please her, and I want to give of myself and enjoy in her delight. I would hope that it is mutual on her end as well, which I'm sure it is. That is what makes a good lover. A good lover is a giver.

Women also want us to share. They want to have a discussion. They want us to speak to them, talk with them, tell them how we feel, and talk about what's going on. Now, some of you may be saying, "Come on, do I really need to do all of that? Do I really need to share my thoughts and feelings?" You know what? The answer is yes! Yes, you do! You may not need to share everything, but women certainly want us to share what's going on and they want to be a part of the story. What story? The one you are creating together; the story God created the two of you for. After all these years of marriage, I've learned (mostly the hard way), that I need to stop, make sure I'm ready to be fully attentive (put the phone away, turn the TV off, etc.) and ask my wife about her day, be ready to listen, and also share what's going on in my world. And yes, be ready for the questions she asks and the details she needs. Men and women were created differently for a reason. There's supposed to be balance and support. We are supposed to complement each other in the journey. I have my strengths and weaknesses, and Trish has different ones, yet many of her strengths support my weaknesses, and vice versa.

Remember that women also want us to have our own lives. There are things that men share with men, which is why having a "band of brothers" is so important. We need men around us that we can go to and say, "Listen, this is what I'm thinking," "I'm a little afraid; let me run this by you," "Tell me what you think," or "Here's what I'm struggling with." That's healthy.

Women want to be a part of the journey and the process. They want to know we can be sensitive and have feelings, and they want us to share those feelings with them. And if we're confident in who we are, where we are going, and what we are doing, then we should also want to know how our partner is doing and how she feels, because we can't accomplish what we want to accomplish together if we don't know where she is at.

CREATORS

Lastly, women want us to be creators. This is one of my favorite subjects to talk about because I think it's such a big misconception with Christian men, and really all men in general. I think we've forgotten who we were created to be.

We were created by God, our Creator, and the Bible says that we are created in the image of our Creator. I want you to really wrap your mind around that for a moment: if we're created in the image of God, our Creator, then we are able to create! Napoleon Hill said in the book *Think and Grow Rich*: *"Whatever the mind of man can believe, and conceive, it can achieve."* Well, who created the mind of man? We'll dive more into this when we discuss goals and goal-setting.

So, what does being a creator in our households really look like? Well, for one, we create our income. Now, you may be thinking, "What are you talking about, John? I don't create my income; somebody else dictates my wage." That's both true and not true. Who chose the job? Who was the one who said yes to the employment? And if you're an entrepreneur, like I am, then you know that you get to create your income every day. A provider is a creator. We are going to touch on the power of that in the next chapter, but understand this: we are only limited by what we believe is possible. In his book *Secrets of the Millionaire Mind*, T. Harv Eker discusses the topic of the "money thermostat" in great detail. I highly recommend you read that book (and all the books I reference).

As husbands and fathers, we're creating all the time. We are creating the relationships we have with our wives, and we're also creating the relationships we have with our children. We get to choose what kind of husbands and fathers we want to be.

I'll share a story with you that's very near and dear to me.

We have two children, Sofia (age nineteen) and Ethan (age fifteen). I always knew I wanted to be a father, and I wanted to be an incredible one. It was a personal mission of mine to be the very best father I could be. I wanted very much to be an engaged dad. I didn't want to miss out on anything. That was part of the reason we gave everything up and moved to Florida. I knew that if we didn't, I would miss out on so much. Both of our children require different things at different times. My relationship with both of them means so very much to me. The fact that we have a daughter and a son is a true blessing.

I adore my daughter very much, and the relationship that we have is very, very special. I remember when Sofia started to develop physically, and she said, "Look, Daddy, look what's happening."

In that moment, I had to make a decision. Was I going to be checked out or was I going to check in? Was I going to be fully present and look at my little girl on her way to becoming a woman, or was I just going to try to ignore it?

I chose to jump in and revel with her in her development and maturity. I chose to celebrate it with her and continued to be there throughout the entire process.

I created that relationship with my daughter, and I cherish it the same way I cherish my relationship with our son Ethan. I understand that he's looking at me the way I looked at my dad when I was young. I create that father-son bond—that passing of the baton, the bestowing of leadership, maturity, and responsibility.

I'm not going to be an absent dad; I'm not going to be a workaholic. I'm going to be there. I create that relationship. You have the power to create those relationships.

How do we want our children to leave us?

After all, they're going to leave. Tricia and I are dealing with that right now. How do we handle developing our children as leaders so they can go out and impact the world (preferably, in a far greater way than we did)? We're not here by accident. We're here for a reason and a purpose. If you're a father, then the opportunity that you have, the gift that you've been given by God, to bestow this passing of the baton and teach your children how to be leaders and move the world forward is an incredible one! I mean, think about what an awesome, incredible responsibility that is. We get to create that. If you have young kids (or want them in the future), close your eyes right now, clear your mind, and picture them. Now, ask yourself: "What kind of people do I want them to be?"

From the moment our children were born, Trish and I parented them based upon the adults we wanted them to be. Who they are today, the people they've become, is not some random accident. It was by design. The main reason Trish and I gave everything up and moved to Florida was because we knew what we wanted for our children, and how it would impact their development. We completely transformed our lives to make that happen.

Again, this goes back to goals. If you haven't picked up on it yet, everything is about goals, goals, and goals. Goal-setting is that important! Decide what kind of people you want your children to be, then create that with them.

Now, children have their own bent, right? God makes them in a certain way, right? Yes, that is true, but they are greatly influenced by the things we teach and show them. They are influenced by the things we say and the things we do. So, be the leader. Be confident. Be the man that creates an incredible life for your wife and children.

In order to do that, we are going to have to spend some time learning the creative process.

CHAPTER 5

CREATED IN THE IMAGE OF A CREATOR

One of the most powerful and life-changing lessons I've learned in my journey so far is discovering how powerful the human mind really is. When I share with you that God created us to be creators, I'm not being melodramatic. It's true. So true, in fact, that I'd consider it the difference between living and existing. Or better yet, the difference between living a life of purpose and intent and merely *surviving.*

We're about to dive into some technical stuff—some things that you really need to know in order to understand how our brains operate and how powerful God created them to be.

Proverbs 23:7 (KJV) states, *"As a man thinketh in his heart, so is he."* So, what is God saying to us? This means our head and heart have to be in alignment. God is referring to goals; and not just theoretical goals, but *emotional* goals! You see, it's not enough to just think of things. How many times have you thought of things you wanted or would like to see happen, but never saw come to fruition? This occurs when our thoughts aren't aligned with our heart. And our hearts carry our emotions. If we aren't emotionally connected to the things we really want, they simply become wishes, not wants!

Here's an example: You could say, "*It would be nice to have $_____ dollars*" or "*I would really love to have this house,*" but if you're not emotionally connected to the goal, you're just not going to do what's necessary to obtain it.

Now, let's say you are going to be short on your rent or your mortgage payment. Your mortgage company is threatening to foreclose or your landlord is going to evict you. You have to make the payment, right? You know that if you don't, you are jeopardizing your family's living situation. I think you'd agree that you will pretty much do whatever you have to do to make that payment. Why is that? Because you are *emotionally* connected to the result!

We were created with two minds: the conscious and the subconscious. Our conscious mind is the ever-present mind. The conscious mind is the one we know, the one we hear and listen to. The conscious mind is the mind that develops beliefs, which are either positive or negative, true or untrue. These beliefs can also be called "agreements" (we agree that this is true and this is not, etc.). Our beliefs are very, very powerful. Our beliefs are the things that define us. They're the things that choose the course of our destiny. One person can believe that they will earn $100,000, and another person can have a hard time believing they'll earn $1000. It's not an ability thing; it's a thought thing—a belief thing. I promise you this: if the person who doesn't believe they can earn a thousand dollars were to get emotionally tied to earning $100,000, they would absolutely hit that goal if they continued to stay emotional, put in the work, and stay positive about hitting it.

Our subconscious mind is the mind that's always working for us behind the scenes. It's the subconscious mind that works to prove the conscious mind right. Again, I'll give you an example: if we say, *"I'm a failure," "I'm a loser,"* or *"I can't do this,"* then the subconscious mind says, *"Hey, what do we have to do to prove this is true?"* The subconscious mind is working all the time. It never takes a day off.

Now, think about what you're really thinking about all day long, because we certainly do a lot of thinking. We've got to look at our beliefs and what we're saying, because God created our brain to work in this manner. We have our thoughts, and the subconscious mind works to prove them right.

The second thing that's equally important about our brain is that it makes a very clear distinction between survival and goals. In fact, if we don't have goals, then our brain is only going to do whatever is necessary to survive.

Let me give that to you again in a different way. The conscious mind has thoughts and beliefs, and if the conscious mind is only thinking about survival ("I've got to pay this bill," "I've got to meet this deadline," "I've got to get the kids here," "I've got to do this," "She wants that," etc.), then all our subconscious mind is going to do is make sure it keeps us surviving.

Maybe you're wondering why life isn't progressing for you the way you thought it would. The great battles and adventures that you thought of as a kid—why aren't they playing out? Why are you living this life of mediocrity? The answer is because most of your thoughts are probably survival thoughts. They're probably thoughts on things that are day-to-day tasks and routines, and we're so inundated with those tasks and routines that we're not moving forward.

That was me. I was that guy. I was so caught up in being a band director, and so caught up in the next task, the next project. When I came home there were chores, as well as tending to what my wife and kids needed. All of that was an endless loop of survival. There was no time for goals. This went on day after day, week after week, year after year. And it never stopped!

I call that the "hamster wheel of life." That's not living. There's no power or purpose; there's no enemy or crusade. There's nothing, and God didn't create us for that. He didn't want us to live a life like that. Society may want us to, but not God.

Now, let's inject goals into the equation. When there are goals, the brain has something to focus on. It doesn't matter what the goal is, as long as *it's emotional!* It could be:

- I'm going to raise my income.

- I'm going to take this vacation with my family.

- I'm going to write a book.

- I'm going to have this car.

- I'm going to have this house.

The important thing is that you have emotional goals. What about a goal to be the best father you can be, the best husband you can be, or the best friend you can be? The bottom line is this: start setting goals. I believe fully that whenever we start moving forward in a positive direction towards a big goal, mission, purpose, or crusade, then the universe moves in our favor as well. As we have evolved as a species, we have created some pretty incredible things. Life is about moving forward. It's expanding, growing, and increasing. Look at all the things we can do today, and the little things we take for granted—things like a cell phone, which was once just a dream in a human being's head. Today, it's commonplace.

Goals are vitally important, but most men don't have any real ones. They're afraid to really go after their dreams because they're taught to accept mediocrity. I can't tell you how many times people tell me they want to be "comfortable." I often hear, "I don't want to be rich or anything, I just want to be comfortable," which is such a lie! Don't you want to have abundance and help your family prosper? Don't you want to travel the world and see God's incredible creation firsthand? Of course you do! And there is nothing wrong with wanting to be financially independent. Ask most people when they would like to not have to wake up and go to work, and they'll tell you, "Tomorrow!"

Society is leading us to believe that having goals and dreams is "unrealistic" and we should be happy with mediocrity. Look at the statistics I shared earlier; men are failing. Why? Because I believe that if you ask a man to just survive, at some point, he's going to rebel. Men need a crusade and a cause. They need a purpose and a clear enemy. Just look at sports and the attraction to it. The team in the "wrong" jersey is the enemy, and we want to take out the enemy.

The purpose can be to take care of a wife and family, which is such a great purpose. Wanting to have a family, fight for that family, make that family prosper, and be the man that family is proud of, the father our sons looks up to, and the man our daughters measure every other man to is so important. It's so incredibly noble and, well… "manly!"

Back in 2005, I learned something that was a true game-changer: the reason most people (including me) were stuck in their lives. Most people are simply thinking about goal achievement the wrong way. We think, "If I have this, then I could do this, and I would be this." That's how we approach our life. "When I have this, I can do this, and I'll be this"—but that's not really how it works. How it really works is: "If I can be this, then I could do this, and I'll have this."

BE, DO, HAVE

Let's say your goal is to be a great husband. You can sit down and say, "Okay, what does a great husband look like?" Come up with all of the qualities that make up a great husband and make a conscious decision to BE them. You will then DO the things that type of person does. The next thing you know, you will HAVE this incredible marriage and incredible relationship with your spouse.

You can make the powerful choice to apply that right now in any area of your life! God created you that way.

I want to share a story with you that's very tough for me to reveal publicly, but it's an area most men will struggle with in some fashion. I also want you to get that I'm not writing from some lofty perch high up in the "look how great I am" tower. No, my friend, I'm a real guy who's walked through some real heavy stuff.

I had a porn addiction, and a really bad one. The statistics I shared earlier, with you? Yeah, I was that guy.

I would download videos and save them. I'm

not proud of it, but it's true. When we left our life in Connecticut and moved to Florida, I had a box of video tapes and DVDs. It was in the garage, and one night, God spoke to me very clearly in a vision. He said, "I will not bless you unless you break that addiction and throw that stuff out!" It was very, very clear, and at three o'clock in the morning, I woke up, went into the garage, grabbed the box of porn, and put it in the trash.

I had to break free of that addiction. I would love to tell you that it was cured quickly, but that addiction followed me for years until I got emotionally connected to what it really was, how detrimental it was to my life, and the idea that I truly no longer wanted to be a statistic. I had to be a stronger man. I had to become a man that was free of it.

I had to reframe the addiction. I had to make sure I was being a man free of that addiction in my head. I started to do the right things, and I eventually broke that habit.

By the way, the attack from pornography will come to most men when they are alone, bored, and inactive. When no one's around, no one's watching. I had to find things to keep myself busy and preoccupied even when I was alone. I now teach my son how not to fall into that trap, which goes back to being the creator of our house and being in charge of our children.

No matter where you are and what you're dealing with, you can make a conscious decision to BE the person you want to be. You will then DO the things that person does. Then, my friend, you will HAVE what that person has. It's that simple. Easy? Nope! But simple. Besides, nothing easy is really worth it.

I shared in the introduction that we are called as men to lead our family, finances, and businesses with faith. In the space provided, write out a description of what your ideal family life, financial life, and career life would look like. Get as visual and emotional as possible. That's the first step, so don't short-change yourself and put parameters on. Take the gloves off! If you could have these ideals any way you'd like, what would they be?

My relationship with my spouse would look like this:

_____

_____

_____

_____

_____

_____

My relationship with my children would look like this:

_____

_____

_____

_____

_____

My ideal financial life would be:

_____

_____

_____

_____

_____

My ideal career would be:

_____

_____

_____

_____

_____

_____

Congratulations! For some of you, this may be the very first time you've done something that specific! I was forty years old when I did it, and it literally changed my life!

I hope you are really getting that these things have incredible power when applied positively in your life.

CHAPTER 6

CREATED FOR PURPOSE

A while ago, I was in church and the pastor asked the congregation, "How many of you have read the Old Testament?" The response floored me. Only about ten to fifteen percent of the people raised their hands. I was saddened to see so many people missing out on such depth and passion. I have a deep love for the Old Testament of the Bible. It contains incredible stories and a rich history. I truly believe it's the first half of an incredible love story between God and men. Among those stories is a great story of manhood, and it's found in the book of Joshua.

If you don't already know, Joshua was the second-in-command to Moses. I'm sure you're familiar with the story of Moses. Moses was an Israelite, raised in an Egyptian household, only to then flee Egypt and spend the next forty years living in the land of Midian as a sheep herder. He was then called by God to lead the

Jews out of Egypt.

Once freed from Egypt, God has to make sure the Jews are ready in their hearts and minds to take control of the Promised Land. He tasks Moses with their leadership and preparation. This goes on for some time; in fact, what should have been a twelve-day journey becomes one of forty years. Finally, the Jews are camped just outside of the promised land. Moses passes away and Joshua is next in line. Moses was the leader everyone followed and looked up to. For forty years, he was the figurehead, and now Joshua is passed the mantle of leadership. Naturally, Joshua is a bit nervous to fill such big sandals!

In Joshua 1:5 (NKJV), God says to him, *"No man shall be able to stand before you all the days of your life as I was with Moses, so will I be with you. I will not leave you nor forsake you. Be strong and of good courage, for to this people you shall divide as an inheritance the land which I swore to their fathers to give them. Only be strong and very courageous, that you may observe to do all according to all the law which Moses My servant commanded you; do not turn from it to the right hand or to the left."*

Then, he says to him in Joshua 1:9 (NKJV): *"Have I not commanded you? Be strong and of good courage; do not be afraid, nor be dismayed, for the Lord your God is with you wherever you go."*

God is calling Joshua to his mission, and I believe that as men, we are wired by God to have our own crusade, our own cause—something bigger than ourselves that we can commit to. I believe we have to have an enemy to take on, something that is the antithesis of what we are and what we believe in, and we have to have a major purpose. Our lives have to mean something.

This is the great task of Joshua. He has to lead the Jews into a foreign territory, and more importantly, he's got to clean it out. Can you imagine the task ahead of him? This is what his whole life has led up to. We're not talking about dusting and vacuuming, and we're not talking about exterminating bugs; we're talking about cleaning out people who have totally disrespected God! They've gone against Him, and He's basically saying, "Joshua, I'm going to need you to fight a war that will define your life. This is your purpose, your calling. I'm going to need you to go to battle, Joshua. I'm going to need you to kill all of these people, in my name, to cleanse the land."

The idea of that astounds me.

We spend a lot of time talking about Noah. Everyone knows the story of Noah! Noah had to deal with a flood that wiped out all of humanity, but Noah didn't have to personally commit genocide. Joshua and the people of Israel were the ones that had to go out and take their territory. It was their calling. It was their crusade.

They had a very clear enemy: the Hittites, the Girgashites, the Amorites, the Canaanites, the Perizzites, the Hivites, and the Jebusites. These made up "Seven nations that are greater and stronger than you!" This is their great purpose.

They are brought here for this reason. It is also the reason God had to wipe out a generation of people for forty years before they entered the Promised Land. He knew they did not believe in Him, nor did they believe in themselves. They were slaves, and because they were slaves, they lost sight of their purpose.

It was the next generation that was ready to go, so Joshua leads them into the Promised Land and fights the major battle that absolutely changes the course of history.

If you look at the Old Testament from Abraham to Moses, from Moses delivering Israel out of Egypt to Joshua, and from Joshua to David, you will find story upon story of men rising up and fighting a battle, having a purpose and a very clear enemy. They are doing this because they are called up to do so!

Joshua fights to cleanse the land, but because they don't get everybody out, war continues to break out over and over again. Here, you have the great heroes of the Bible—men like Gideon, Samson, Samuel, King Saul, and finally David. What's interesting when we get to David is that David finally wins the battles and sets up the kingdom.

Though he wasn't perfect, God does say of David that he was "a man after my own heart."

There is a major lesson here: God calls David a man after his own heart, yet David was a murderer and an adulterer. What's the point? It's that we don't have to be perfect. Society is trying to get us to be perfect when we're not. We fall way short of it. We are not supposed to be perfect on purpose!

We'll talk about that a little bit later, but for a moment, pause and realize that you don't have to be this perfect guy. You don't have to have it all figured out. We're going to make mistakes, and we're going to screw it up. We do that. We're men, but we are still called to the plans and purposes of God.

Something very interesting happens after David sets up the kingdom. David had many sons, but Solomon is the one who inherits the kingdom. When we speak of Solomon, we mostly speak of his wisdom and his wealth. We talk of his major accomplishments, but we rarely talk about how Solomon ultimately failed God. How did he fail? When Solomon inherits the kingdom, most of the major wars are over and he inherits most of the wealth. Let me be very clear: I'm not diminishing one of the greatest kings to ever walk the earth. The point I'm making is that Solomon's major calling was in prospering Israel, but he got so wrapped up in the trappings of success that it led him away from God. He didn't have a crusade, there was no clear enemy, and he lost sight of his purpose.

People would come from all over the world to see his kingdom. He had 700 wives and 300 concubines. Ultimately, Solomon drifted, and his drifting split the kingdom in two and led to its downfall. Israel was never the same.

Another more modern version of this story took place during World War II, with what we now call the Greatest Generation. If you are in your forties, like me, this included our grandparents. My grandfather, who is long gone now, had a picture of himself sitting at a makeshift desk in France about to get on a train to go to Normandy. He was young and filled with promise. Before him was a crusade, a very clear enemy, and a major purpose. His generation, the greatest generation, had to rise up and face the challenge. If you watch movies set in this time period, you see men saying things like, "I cannot stand by and watch. I have to go. I have to be a part of this." Most knew they were not coming back. This sense of purpose is wired into us. We have to have an enemy.

Why is this so important? Because we don't act in comfort. Enemies define our circumstance. Maybe the enemy today is your financial life. Maybe you're sick and tired of where you're at financially and want to change it. Do you want to know the real enemy in society today, in our world of advanced technology, handheld computers, and instant gratification? The real enemy is mediocrity. Mediocrity will take you out! I've heard it said that the enemy of "great" is "good." A lot of people are okay being "good." I'm not even sure what that really means. What does "I'm good" mean? That you've "got yours?" That you're all set? If you have all your basic needs set, does that mean there is no other reason to go after more? I cannot, nor ever will, relate to that standpoint.

The World War II generation was going to stand up and fight, and they were committed to changing their global circumstances. They knew they had to do something about it. They couldn't deny it. It transcended them.

What is our great purpose today? Think about it. If you were to pause and ask yourself, "What's my great purpose?", what would it be? Is it money? Is that a really great purpose—the chasing of money? In the end, if money is your purpose, you'll find that it's empty and meaningless.

Is it position, or a title? I promise you that if you're chasing position and title, there is something else missing. The position or the title is a cover-up. Unfortunately, when we achieve these things, we find that the main problem is still there.

I found that out in my pursuit of one of the main positions in my business. For three years, I was consumed by it. Nothing else really mattered except getting to this position. I've now been at this position for many years, and looking back on it, it was the battle to get there that's most memorable. The struggle. The pain. All of the defeat along the way. Why? Because there was a cause, an enemy, and a purpose! They were there. Yes, they were small in the grand scheme of things, but they were there!

Are you chasing cars or chasing homes? Is our great purpose just to wake up every day? To get a nice car, have a nice home, have a great title, and have a lot of money? Unfortunately, in our society today, that's how we're defined.

Just go out there on Instagram and Facebook. You will see a constant barrage of "I'm taking this trip," "I'm driving this car," "Look at how great my house is," or "Look at how great my life is." All of this is well and good, but it's not the major purpose God calls us to. This is not what God wires us for, and it's not why you were born.

Money, position, and possessions are not important. There's a bigger battle to fight: the Great Battle. The battle for Him, for God. The battle for the things that He stands for and why He created us. The things that are good, honest, true, and right in the world. Trust me, there is a spiritual battle with a real enemy, a real cause, and a real crusade!

I believe God creates men to stand on "Four Pillars," which are the core elements of this book. He needs men of Integrity, Humility, Authenticity, and Morality. These are the "Four Pillars."

If we don't stand on them, then the consequences will be more of the statistics we discussed earlier. If we don't stand in our integrity, humility, authenticity, and morality, we have a more likely shot of getting divorced, committing adultery, creating single-parent homes, becoming addicted to pornography and drugs, and committing more gun violence. That's not what we want, so we've got to learn how to stand on these "pillars" at home and in the marketplace.

THE FOUR PILLARS

CHAPTER 7

PILLAR ONE: INTEGRITY

<u>INTEGRITY</u>

"The quality of being honest and having strong moral principles." That's the dictionary definition of integrity. Another definition I read defined integrity as "being true to yourself." If we are going to live and lead at home and in our workplace, then integrity is a must! I truly believe integrity is about staying true to your word. It's about doing what you say you are going to do. If you say you're going to do something, then do it.

I want to illustrate integrity in the Bible with two great stories, then share a personal one.

<u>JOSEPH</u>

The first biblical story comes from the Book of Genesis. It's the story of Joseph. If you don't know the story, Joseph had many brothers and he was his father's favorite. His brothers knew this, but it wasn't a major issue until the day Joseph was anointed by God through a dream, which put him ahead of his brothers. Joseph chooses to share his dream with his brothers, who then become so upset with him that they sell him into slavery, faking his death, and lie to their father. Joseph finds himself in a situation where life has turned quickly from prosperity to slavery.

Joseph, amidst serious, life-changing circumstances, could easily have whined, complained, or quit, but he doesn't. Joseph never stops being who he is: a man with a high degree of integrity. As a matter of fact, Joseph had all the qualities we're going to talk about in this book, but for this example, I want to illustrate his level of integrity. Joseph had a "moral steadfastness." He was firm in his beliefs, and he was honest.

Joseph rises through the ranks of his master's household and eventually becomes head of the household. The Bible says that God was with Joseph and God blessed him, and therefore, his master was also blessed.

In Genesis 39:7-9 (NKJV), we find Joseph facing a difficult decision:

"And it came to pass after these things that his master's wife cast longing eyes on Joseph and she said, 'Lie with me.' But he refused and said to his master's wife, 'Look, my master does not know what is with me in the house, and he has committed all that he has to my hand. There is no one greater in this house than I, nor has he kept back anything from me but you, because you are his wife. How then can I do this great wickedness and sin against God?'"

Joseph is saying, "Look, I have everything in my master's house except you, because you're his wife. I cannot do this, and please don't ask this of me." He knows that if he is to continue being blessed, he must stand in his integrity.

The Bible goes on in Genesis 39:10 (NKJV), *"So it was as she spoke to Joseph day by day, that he did not heed her, to lie with her or to be with her."*

Every day she came at him, and every day, he replied with, "Look, this is not going to happen."

Genesis 39:11 (NKJV) explains, *"But it happened about this time, when Joseph went into the house to do his work, and none of the men of the house was inside, that she caught him by his garment, saying, 'Lie with me.' But he left his garment in her hand, and fled and ran outside."*

If you are familiar with the story, then you know she goes on to frame him. As she is holding his garment, she tells everybody that he tried to rape her and Joseph is thrown into prison. Yet Joseph never wavers in his integrity.

Are we as men today standing in our integrity?

Maybe your own struggles don't involve adultery. Maybe they involve being asked to do something at work that doesn't line up with your moral and ethical values. Or maybe at home or in the office, you gave your word that you would get a certain thing done. Do you do what you say you're going to do, or do you find yet another reason to not come through? I can't tell you how many men I've met and worked with who will say whatever they need to say to make themselves look good, but never really come through. The sad thing is that they are compromising their integrity. The message to everyone around them is "We can't count on you" and "Your word isn't worth much." I find this to be incredibly sad. What we don't realize is that by compromising our word, we set in motion actions and events that will never work out in our favor, and prosperity cannot be achieved long-term.

DAVID

I referred to David earlier, and there is so much to learn from his story. When David was young, Saul was the anointed king. Saul, being selfish and insecure, never fully trusted God, and God decided to choose another, David, to build the kingdom of Israel. David was anointed king while still under the rule of Saul. It would have been very easy for him to start acting in that position of leadership, calling out Saul and his family, but he didn't. David believed in his heart that Saul was "The Lord's Anointed," and would not take arms against Saul, even though Saul was trying to kill him.

We see an incredible example of integrity in 1 Samuel, Chapter 24. In this portion, David is hiding in a cave and Saul is looking for him.

Saul, not knowing David and his men are hiding in a certain cave, goes into the cave to relieve himself. As Saul is taking care of his business, David quietly sneaks up and cuts off a piece of Saul's robe. Saul leaves the cave, and David steps out and calls out to him:

"'My lord the king!' And when Saul looked behind him, David stooped with his face to the earth, and bowed down." (I Samuel 24:8 NKJV)

David is in a position of humility.

"And David said to Saul, "Why do you listen to the words of men who say, 'Indeed David seeks you harm?' Look, this day your eyes have seen that the Lord delivered you today into my hand in that cave, when someone urged me to kill you. But my eye spared you, and I said, 'I will not stretch out my hand against my lord, for he is the Lord's anointed.' Moreover, my father, see! Yes, see the corner of your robe in my hand! For in that I cut off the corner of your robe, and did not kill you, know and see that there is neither evil nor rebellion in my hand, and I have not sinned against you. Yet you hunt my life to take it. Let the Lord's judge between you and me, and let the Lord avenge me on you. But my hand shall not be

against you." (I Samuel 24:9-12 NKJV)

What a powerful example of integrity. I mean, think about it: David had every right to take out Saul. David was running for his life, living in caves in the wilderness, hunted down by the man he dedicated his life to. He had every right, especially in his men's eyes, to take out Saul, but he didn't because he swore an allegiance to him. He does what he says he's going to do, because he knows that if he doesn't do it, he will displease God.

David's purpose is bigger than Saul. Refer back to what we discussed earlier—we've got to have a crusade, something to fight for. For David, fighting for his God and keeping his integrity was a much bigger crusade than overcoming Saul. And so, even though he's running for his life and living in caves, he would rather stand in his integrity than compromise it with God.

Again, we may not see something like that happen from day to day, but look at the moments that our integrity comes into play. We've got to do what we say we're going to do, and we've got to do it with the people that are most important to us.

The first person that should be most important to you is YOU. Yes, "mighty warrior," I'm talking to you! You're the person. You've got to have integrity with yourself first!

When you're riding in an airplane and the oxygen mask comes down, you're supposed to put that on yourself first. Why? Because if you don't save yourself first, you won't be alive to save anybody else. Similarly, you have to honor yourself with integrity.

I was taught early on by some incredible mentors that there are five things in our lives that we've got to have: faith, family, fitness, finances, and fun. Well, do you have integrity with your own faith? Do you say one thing and do another? Do you make promises to God and not keep them? What about your fitness? Do you say you're going to work out but don't?

Here's a great example: you say you're going to work out tomorrow morning, but when the alarm goes off, you hit the snooze button, roll over, and go back to sleep. When you do that, you've compromised your integrity with yourself! And when you compromise your integrity with yourself, you're pretty much giving yourself permission to keep doing it. If we do that on a continuous basis, we can never live a life of passion and purpose. How you do one thing is how you do everything.

Do we have integrity in our finances? Are our finances in order? Are we putting money in the proper places? Are we upholding our integrity?

Another issue I struggled with for a long time is having integrity with our fun. I believed that if I didn't keep working, working, working, I was going to fail.

Life isn't just about work. You have to have something to relieve the pressure. Have integrity with your fun. If you say you're going to go hit golf balls because you've been working hard all week, go hit golf balls! Have the integrity with yourself to go do that. If you say you're going to take some time and go to the beach or read a book, have the integrity with yourself to go do it. Again, this was a major area of struggle for me. I believed everyone else deserved it but me, and would find myself feeling guilty for allowing myself to have fun. My friends, colleagues, and mentors would all point it out, but I didn't want to believe it. I was programmed that success only came from continuous hard work, and I bought into a belief that until success was reached, having fun wasn't permitted. What a lonely and sad existence that can be. Don't let that be you. Have the integrity to have fun. Make it a strong moral principle. Now, I'm not saying to use it as an excuse. You would then be out of integrity!

HAVING INTEGRITY WITH OUR WIVES

I stated earlier that I would give you a personal example of standing in integrity. This one was extremely tough.

During my "Desert Year," Trish and I were trying to figure out where our relationship stood, but I knew I was going to hurt her. One night, while we were watching a movie, Trish turned her head and looked into my eyes. Here was this beautiful woman in my lap, staring longingly at me, knowing that she wanted to spend her life with me, and I knew I was seriously screwed up in the head.

I knew I was going to hurt her and that if she stayed with me, I was going to compromise my integrity. I knew I was going to display bad character. I knew I was going to do a lot of things that went against the man I wanted to be. Trish must have picked up on the fact that something was off, because she said, "Do you even want to be with me?" In that moment, I couldn't compromise. Even though I knew it was going to hurt her and possibly hurt our friendship forever, I needed to do the tough thing. I looked into those beautiful brown eyes and said, "No. I can't right now." And I crushed her.

That's integrity.

I'm not boasting here. I'm telling you that I knew what I had to do to maintain integrity, and I did it.

We've got to have integrity with our wives. When we say to our wives, "I will fight for you," we've got to fight for them in all kinds of moments and scenarios. We've got to stand up for them. We've got to make sure that society doesn't try to pull our marriages apart. We've got to have the integrity to stand there and do what we said we were going to do when we said "Till death do us part." We've got to fight and have the integrity to not let mediocrity take us out.

What does mediocrity look like today?

Well, in today's digital world, it's found in our "smart" phones, social media, Netflix, and apps. Those things foster mediocrity. We've got to lead, and we've got to stand. We've got to tell our wives "I will stand for you," "I will be with you," and "I will fight for you."

EXERCISE

In the space below, write down the answer to the following question:

How can I keep my integrity with my wife?

_____

_____

_____

_____

_____

_____

HAVING INTEGRITY WITH OUR CHILDREN

This is an area that I am extremely passionate about.

It's our job to provide for our children. It's an honor and a privilege to do so. It's not our job to make them figure it out. They weren't responsible for their birth; we were—just as we weren't responsible for our own; our parents were. Our children are our responsibility, and we honor them by leading them, providing for them, and teaching them to do the same. There's a great song by the group Sanctus Real called "Lead Me" that does a great job of illustrating the thoughts and feelings of our children:

"Lead me with strong hands.

Stand up when I can't.

Don't leave me hungry for love

Chasing dreams, but what about us?

Show me you're willing to fight

That I'm still the love of your life

I know we call this our home

But I still feel alone."

We have to have enough integrity with our children to say, "I will honor you." What does honoring our children look like? We have to honor the people they will be. Our children need to know that we will be there for them, and that we honor them and value them.

Think about a child who knows their parents value who they are and what they think. When a child knows that their parents honor them, they know they can go to them and trust them.

We have to have integrity with our time and spend time with our children. As a new father, or one with young kids, you can read to them at night, sing to them, hold them, and spend time with them. Turn off the TV, turn off the apps, get your head out of your iProducts, and spend time with them.

Imagine the child that goes to sleep every night after having their father hug them, hold them, and tell them how much they love them. Don't miss the power of that!

We have to honor our children by saying, "I will guide you; I will take the time to lead you, guide you, be there for you, and be your father, mentor, and coach." Have the integrity to stand firm for your children, and more importantly, have the integrity to be an example for them every day. Our children are watching. They're watching the men that we are. They're watching because they want to see who we are, what we do, and how we live our lives. Be that example. Remember, you are the creator!

EXERCISE

In the space below, write down the answer to the following question:

How can I keep my integrity with my children?

_____

_____

_____

_____

_____

_____

INTEGRITY IN THE MARKETPLACE

The number one way I think we compromise our integrity at work is in the area of time management. Have the integrity to be on time. Be early. This was an area I suffered greatly in. I had a major time issue. I was consistently ten minutes late, so much so that a dear friend and mentor of mine would say, "That's Puritz Time." "Puritz Time" meant ten minutes late. We would be in a meeting, and he would say, "Okay, everybody, the meeting is at 7:00. But for John, it's at 6:50 because he's on 'Puritz Time.'" I got so fed up with him saying that, I made up my mind to never be late again. Today, I hold time and the respect of it in high value. I am not late.

Have the integrity to be on time. Have the integrity to be fully present during the times that we need to. Darren Hardy does a great talk on multitasking on YouTube. Sitting in one meeting and looking at our phones is not multitasking. It's not being present.

Have the integrity to bring your whole self to the moment that you're in. When you're at work and you're working, be fully present and engaged. When you're in a meeting, be fully present and engaged. When you're in conversation, be fully present and engaged. Have the integrity of presence.

Finally, have the integrity at work to deliver on your value. You know what your value is, and you know what you bring to the table. Deliver that value. Have the integrity to give your full self and your full value, then overshoot that value.

In the great book *The Science of Getting Rich*, Wallace Wattles says, *"Give more in use value than you receive in cash value."* I've tried to live that out as much as possible. No, we will never be perfect, but it's the daily intent to be the best we can be that matters.

EXERCISE

In the space below, write down the answer to the following question:

How can I keep my integrity at work and in the marketplace?

_____

_____

_____

MAN UP, ALREADY!

_____

_____

_____

CHAPTER 8

PILLAR TWO: HUMILITY

HUMILITY

Humility is defined as "a modest or low view of one's own importance." I think the idea of being humble has been misconstrued in our society today. When we say a man is humble, what picture comes to mind? A strong man? Probably not. We tend to think humility equates to weakness. That's typically how society portrays a humble person.

We also tend to think that humility represents a lack of self-respect, and that couldn't be farther from the truth. Ask yourself this: can you have complete and total self-respect, acknowledging your own self-worth, and at the same time, understand that your importance to others isn't as great as it may be to yourself?

We spend so much time out in the world

trying to validate our importance to others. We can be incredibly self-absorbed. Humility, on the other hand, is about having enough self-confidence to not have to seek validation from others, and therefore be able to *be* about others. Our importance to ourselves is simply not that important to others.

There's a great example of this in the Bible, but before I illustrate that point, let me ask you a question: who do you picture in your mind to strap on a sword and go fight a giant like Goliath, David, or Jesus? I think we miss the fierce and mighty warrior that Christ was, and still is. Just look at Jesus's resume up to the last night of his death: he cast out demons, raised a man from the dead, turned water into wine, walked on water, and fed 5,000 people with what appeared to be only enough for five. I think you'd agree that's pretty impressive!

John 13:2 says, *"And supper being ended, Jesus knowing that the Father had given all things into His hand and that he had come from God and was going to God, rose from supper and laid aside His garments took a towel and girded Himself. After that, He poured water into a basin and began to wash the disciples' feet and to wipe them with a towel with which He was girded."*

He has the towel wrapped around himself, and he's wiping and washing their dirty feet. Peter has a hard time accepting this and tries to deny Jesus's gift. Jesus tells him, *"If I do not wash you, you have no part with Me."* When he's finished, Jesus's explanation is the lesson: *"Do you know what I have done for you? You call me teacher and Lord and you say well for I am so. If I then your Lord and teacher have washed your feet, you also ought to wash another's feet for I've given you an example that you should do as I have done to you. Most assuredly I say to you, a servant is not greater than his master nor is he who is sent greater than he who sent him. If you know these things, blessed are you if you do them."*

Look at that picture of humility. The son of God gets on his knees, wraps a towel around himself, and washes the dirty, nasty feet of his followers. I love what Jesus says afterwards: "I have given you a gift and a great example; you need to do this to others." That's humility! True humility is knowing who you are, as well as your strengths and weaknesses. Jesus, the son of God, humbled himself because he understood in that moment that the most important lesson he could teach these men was how to be humble. He could have said, "Hey, I'm Jesus. I'm the son of God! Somebody wash my feet." But He didn't. He did the complete opposite. In my opinion, that's true strength!

What would life be like if you didn't have to spend so much time trying to impress others?

Humility is self-confidence. Humility is being okay with who you are, with absolutely nothing to prove to others. I find it hard enough to prove it to myself. And that is where true self-worth comes from!

Personally, I know I'm a broken man. I know I'm not perfect. I know that I need a savior. It's my brokenness that is the Big Crusade of my life: to know that even though I'm broken, I can get up every day and strive to be a better version of myself. It's hard enough to prove that to myself. It's way more challenging to try to prove it to others. In the end, God loves us regardless!

In my past, I was an egomaniac. I've learned the hard way what not having humility looks like. In my business, humility is a requirement. I learned over time that if we are not humble, people simply won't stay. Whenever you are in a position of leadership, humility is required. In today's marketplace, people have more choices than they've ever had before. They don't have to work where they do. They can find another place. If they are going to stay with us, they have to know that they are valued and respected. Being a humble leader is vital. Every day, I have to ask myself whether or not I'm putting the needs of my people before my own. What's best for our team? What's best for our organization? Will my actions today move us forward for the future? It's all about people, and humility is required. Humility is about giving up your "right to be right." I learned the power of that statement, and it changed my life. Do you know how many relationships, teams, and organizations have fallen apart because someone won't give up their right to be right? It's sad.

How about at home? There tends to be this belief that because we are men, we don't have to do the dishes, clean up after ourselves, or help our wives with the day-to-day chores. That's simply not true. Trish and I have chosen to define our roles and to discuss and plan who does what, instead of assuming it. Sometimes, she needs me to help her in her areas, just as I may need her to help me in mine. Humility is about honoring that request. I don't like certain things, like doing the laundry, but, sometimes I may be called upon to do it (though I still have no idea how to correctly fold the towels!). There are so many little examples and places where these things show up.

Put your ego aside and be humble. I promise you, you will be rewarded—maybe not in that moment, but somewhere down the line. There is something very special about a man who is confident enough in himself to offer that strength in the smallest of ways. It's not all about lifting big, heavy things, or doing the "man" stuff we stereotypically think of. Humility can show up in the smallest of actions, like emptying the dishwasher, wiping down the counter, clearing the drain board, or making dinner.

Be humble. Your own importance is not as important to others. Understand that concept.

<u>EXERCISE</u>

In the blank space below, answer this question:

How can I demonstrate humility at work?

_____

_____

_____

_____

_____

_____

How can I demonstrate humility at home?

_____

_____

_____

_____

_____

CHAPTER 9

PILLAR THREE: AUTHENTICITY

AUTHENTIC: *of undisputed origin; genuine*

AUTHENTICITY: *The quality of being authentic*

Have you ever heard someone refer to another as a "poser?" This means they are giving you one presentation of themselves, but you know that's not the real thing. There is something inauthentic about them. Authenticity is about not having to pose or put on a façade. Authenticity is showing up every day the full person that you are, and being good with it. I've referenced the book *Wild at Heart* many times in this book, and I've shared with you that that book had a major impact on my life. Let me give it a little bit more context.

When I went to my pastor at the time and shared with him all the things I was struggling with, he handed me *Wild at Heart*. During that period of my life, I felt very trapped. I had constructed, as I shared earlier, this façade of a life that I was hiding behind. Every day that I went to work, I would ask myself, "Can I see myself doing this for thirty years?" Could I see myself growing older, going gray, and getting out of shape because I had no time for me personally? It was already happening in my early thirties, and I could see it continuing with no end in sight. My life was passing me by.

I would wrestle with this reality, then drive forty-five minutes to a fifty-year-old home that defined "fixer-upper." Seriously! We would have to shrink-wrap the windows in the winter and install air conditioning units every summer because we didn't have the money to provide the things the house needed, like new windows and central air conditioning. Yet, I would wake up every day, get in the car, drive through traffic, get to work, and teach my students. Some days I'd be in such a foul mood that I didn't want to show up, and to this day I regret how I passed that energy on to my students.

I would grind it out while being one hundred percent inauthentic—not real and genuine to how I felt. When I read *Wild at Heart,* I came across a quote that changed my life.

Eldredge writes, "Let people feel the weight of who you are and let them deal with it." I remember where I was when I read that quote and it cut through so many self-imposed barriers. It was permission for me to be authentic. The real John was going to stand up and speak. I was going to start expressing the things I had a challenge with and the things I didn't want to see in my life. I was going to be authentic.

We discussed earlier that it's when the head and heart connect that real change begins; that when your head and your heart connect, things really start to move. Without getting into details, I found myself in a situation at the high school some time later where I had to stand up for a controversial decision I had made; one I completely still support and would make again. In that moment, I understood that nobody was going to stand with me. I realized neither my principal, the school district, nor anyone else, regardless of what was said, was going to back me up. So there I was, letting people "feel the full weight of who I am," and being extremely authentic. I understood that this awakening was causing me to see how precarious my position was, and how I needed to make a change. I knew that my career choice and position were no longer good for my family.

To tie in the concept of humility—humble men can be authentic men. You can let the world feel the full weight of who you are and let them deal with it, but it can be done with humility. It's not a self-important statement; it's a statement that, again, says, "I am who I am; this is who I am." It's you authentically showing up. It's saying "I know I'm broken. I know I have issues. I know my weaknesses, yet I'm willing to work on them." Humble men can be authentic men, and more importantly, authentic men can be humble men. It's not a standpoint of weakness, but a standpoint of strength.

Biblically, an example of this is the apostle Paul, who was known as Saul during the time of this example. If you don't know Paul's backstory, he was a Jew with the job of imprisoning the Jews that were following a new belief called 'The Way.' The book of Acts tells the story of how Paul, being a Pharisee, was hunting down Jews who had followed the teachings of Jesus.

Paul was very authentic in his Judaism. One day, he was traveling down the Damascus Road, on his way to go capture these people, and he had a moment with God that forever changed him. It was undeniable. It transformed him and reshaped his entire destiny. He could not dispute it or walk away from it. He understood who he was in that moment and was forever changed. He became a follower of Christ instantly. How? He heard from, and spoke with, Jesus. He knew beyond a shadow of doubt and was convicted. And so, he went from authentically being Jew to authentically being a Christian. He stood up and shared his beliefs, even though he knew it was probably going to cost him his life.

Paul took Christianity far beyond the small group that it was in the beginning stages of the faith. Paul, being authentically Christian and at the same time being authentically Jewish, stood in his Judaism, stating, "This is the Messiah!" It's such a great example of standing in authenticity and of knowing who you are, what you're doing, and most importantly, why you are doing it.

Oftentimes, we are going to be called to be

authentic when we are wrong. And that's not
easy!

I want to share another personal story that
taught me a lot while I was going through these
circumstances. As a high school band director, it
was my job to prepare and take our students to
the All-State competition held once every year.
This was the opportunity for our students to
compete with and perform with the best of the
best at their level in the state. This particular
year happened to be the first time we had
students ready for this level of competition, but
my best friend's mother had passed away and
the funeral was held at the same time. Not
wanting to miss being there for my friend, and
authentically standing in that desire, I made
sure all the logistics were taken care of: the
students had chaperones and transportation
was covered. I would meet them as soon as the
funeral, about an hour away, was over.
Everything looked good and in place, or so I
thought.

This was in the early 2000s, so technology
wasn't what it is today. You couldn't do much
with a cell phone except talk on it. Hard to

imagine, I know! It turned out I had forgotten to have our students fill out permission forms, and they couldn't perform without them! I couldn't fax them, email them, or scan them. We were facing a very difficult situation, and it was my fault! Have you ever had a moment where you didn't see the problem coming, and you were sucker-punched in the gut by it? That was me! Thankfully, the chairman of the event allowed our students to finish the day as long as the slips were turned in the next day. I had a long car ride back to the festival, thinking of all the ways I could explain myself to this man, who I was greatly intimidated by. Have you ever had someone in your life who was so good at what they do that you had a hard time trying to play in the same arena? That was me with this guy, and he was the chairman! I felt so incredibly foolish, and I had to meet him and explain myself.

I made a decision on that car ride. I was going, to the best of my ability, to give the greatest explanation I could about what went wrong. I walked in the room, walked up to the table he was sitting at, and said, "I f***ed up!" No better explanation was necessary. He said,

"Hey, we all do it sometimes. Make sure they have those slips tomorrow," and we moved on! I learned a huge lesson that day. Always be authentic. Admit when you are wrong. Let them feel the weight of who you are, good and bad, strengths and flaws. I keep saying this: we are works in progress! We are not perfect. We have flaws. We screw things up. Admit them! Be authentic with them, and strive to be a better version of yourself tomorrow!

That was my marketplace example. How about yours? Are there moments in your past that you can look back on and learn from? How about today? Are there areas that you can look at in your work life and see how you can up your level of authenticity?

In the space provided, answer the question:

How can I be more authentic in my workplace?

_____

_____

_____

_____

_____

An area that needs addressing is being authentic at home, particularly with the women in our lives. This book is titled "Man Up, Already!" for a reason. It's time for men to be authentically men, especially with our women. Now, please don't turn that into some Neanderthal statement. Earlier, I shared with you all of the qualities that women want from us as men. Stand in that authentically! Don't hide behind your woman. She doesn't want that. And if she does, there are probably things that need to be addressed and worked on together. God made men in His image, not hers. There is a natural order to things. Explore it. Discover it. The world needs you to come alive and step into the destiny you were created for. Be authentic. Again, be the man your children measure every man against. The role model your children should be following is you! You should see that as your responsibility, not as a choice. Hey, if that was too harsh, I'm not sorry. Put the book down if it was, because there is a gaping hole in our society that should be filled with strong, authentic men who love God!

In the space provided, answer the following question:

How can I be more authentic at home? What do I need to let go of?

_____

_____

_____

_____

_____

CHAPTER 10

PILLAR FOUR: MORALITY

MORALITY: *Principles concerning the distinction between right and wrong or good and bad behavior.*

The final pillar of "The Four Pillars" is morality. This was very difficult to write about, because I believe morality is a hard thing to define in our society today. Why? Because we see the line between doing what's right and wrong shift so often. We see it in the media, in politics, and in arts and entertainment. We see examples of this shifting line all over the place. Doing what's right is not often what's popular, which is what makes it even more difficult. A couple of days ago, a good friend and colleague of mine was expressing his frustration regarding his work environment. His company was asking him to make promises to a potential client to get them to buy, but then renege on the very same promise after the sale was made. In his spirit, he knew that it was wrong, and he was having a hard time functioning daily to do his job. That's a perfect example of morality: in our spirit, we know the difference between what is right and what is wrong. I truly believe it's wired into us by God.

I want to share another great story in the Old Testament. It takes place 360 years after David, and it concerns a king of Israel named Josiah.

In 2 Kings 22, the Bible reads: *"Josiah was eight years old when he became king. He did what was right in the sight of the Lord and walked in the ways of his father David. He did not turn aside to the right or to the left."*

The backstory to all of this is that for a long, long time, the nations of Israel and Judah (which used to be one kingdom) turned their backs on God, forgetting what He had done for them and his promises to them if they heeded his commandments. "Walked in the ways of his father David" means that Josiah had chosen to follow God the way David did so many years ago. This is important because there was a long line of kings before him who did not follow God's commands. They chose to do what they wanted, influenced by the nations surrounding them—the very same nations God tasked Joshua to clean out.

So, 360 years later, Josiah chooses to model and lead like David. He's about twenty-four years old when he starts to bring about these changes. He removes idols, alters, and priests. He does away with anything against God. Needless to say, this was not popular. Doing right over wrong rarely is. But Josiah had a higher purpose than the people. His crusade and cause, his mission, was to bring the people back into alignment with God. His enemy was anything or anyone that went against that. The Bible states that *"there was no king like him, who turned to the Lord with all his heart, with all his soul, and with all his might, according to all the Law of Moses; nor after him did any arise like him." (2 Kings 23:25)*

I point this story out because of Josiah's extremely high degree of morality. There was a long line of kings before Josiah who were not respecting God. It could have been very easy for him to fall in line. After all, he's only eight years old when he inherits the kingdom. But he doesn't. He's called to a higher standard, and sets an example of doing what's right over wrong; choosing difficult over easy.

Morality at home and in the workplace must be a conscious decision. One of the things I am constantly teaching is the fact that everyone is watching. In case you didn't know that, let me be the first to tell it: everyone is watching! They are watching what you do, the choices you make, and how you react. Every time you do the right thing, you not only give permission for others to do the same, you are also teaching and modeling what it looks like. I truly believe in this social world, where people can craft any message they'd like, displaying a high degree of morality is vital. I'm not talking about coming from a lofty perch, but about displaying morality in the small simple things.

Here's a personal example of what I'm talking about: back in the early 2000s, file sharing started to take off. If you're old enough to remember, there was a company called Napster. Napster introduced, for the first time, the ability to share files of copyrighted music, and it created an absolute uproar. It literally changed the entire music industry. If it weren't for Napster, we might not have what is now Spotify, Apple Music, Pandora, and all the other music sharing programs.

I'm using Napster and file sharing as an example to illustrate a point. Please do not become offended by my point of view or the personal lesson I share. Everything in this book is designed to get you to start thinking about what you are thinking about, and hopefully make some changes where you feel they are needed.

File sharing is still alive and well today. You can pretty much pull anything you want off the internet. But if it's copyrighted, is it right? Now, I was a big supporter of file sharing early on. I looked at it from the point of view that if I had it and was sharing it with someone, it wasn't an issue. It's one thing to own a physical copy, but the digital world changed the game.

When I was a kid, we used to record albums to cassettes. If a friend had a vinyl copy of the music (one they had paid for and purchased), we would give them a cassette tape to record it to. In the analog world, an album or cassette would ultimately warp or wear down, and you'd end up purchasing the recording anyway. The difference in the digital world, especially in the early 2000s, was that the music might have been paid for once, but being shared with millions of people significantly cut into the profits of those that incurred the cost to produce it. It's very easy to say "well, everybody's doing it," but file sharing is an infringement of copyright. Producing the movie or music costs someone money and provides jobs for others. If we're sharing files, we're essentially cutting into that.

Recently, we were given an Amazon Firestick, and if you manipulate it properly, you can install programs that share bootleg copies of movies and, I'm sure, other forms of media. Our son Ethan was so excited to have it, and I found myself being caught up in his excitement. Family movie night is a big thing in our house. We all love movies, and here was this little device that could bring any movie right to our home screen. I mean, that's incredible, right? Well, I said earlier that someone's always watching, and in that moment, it was our children. I knew it was an infringement of copyright law and I was trying to teach my children right from wrong. I had to explain my thoughts to Ethan, and we got rid of the Firestick. The best part of this story is that he got it. He listened and understood. I also went onto iTunes and rented the movie we wanted to watch so he could see my response to the lesson. $5.99 was worth the lesson!

Right now, you must have a point of view on this topic. There appears to be no clear line of right or wrong, right? Well, what does your gut tell you? If you spent your hard-earned money to create, produce, and distribute a product, then found out everyone was getting it for free, how would you feel about that? That's the question. I personally used to download a ton of music and movies, until one day a friend asked me that question. It forced me to look at what was truly right or wrong. It wasn't about my opinion regarding the legality. He asked me what my gut told me, and that was where the answer lied. Since that day, I have paid for what I download. Why? Because my kids are watching, and because if I compromise here, I will compromise in many other places in my life. How you do one thing is how you do everything. That is an absolute fact.

I've heard it said that in today's world, everybody has their own morality. Remember this is defined as a distinction between right and wrong. I truly believe God speaks to us in our gut, through our conscience. Again, I believe it's wired into us.

What about at work? Do we always do the right thing? How easy is it to fudge something here or manipulate a little there? I've seen people in business chase recognition and move the line of right versus wrong to win things that don't really matter in the grand scheme of life. Why do they do that? Because, like Josiah in his time, people choose to chase idols more than they choose to chase God and who He created them to be.

When we're chasing idols, we do things to bypass the system or cut corners so that we can grab that idol, that recognition, that thing we think will bring us gratification; but it never really satisfies long-term. In the Book of Ecclesiastes, Solomon (the man that had it all) says that is all "vapor, and the chasing of the wind." That's what "things" tend to do: provide instant gratification and a false sense of self-worth. In the early stages of my career, I believed those were the things that mattered, and yet, I found myself always looking for more, trying to find that ever-present, elusive thing. It was only when I was at rock bottom with a lot of plaques, trophies, trips, and shirts that I learned where the real value lies: love, gratitude, family, and relationships, to name just a few. That's why the Four Pillars are so important.

Idols can come in many shapes and forms. They are things that we worship. Money, success, sex. You name it, it's out there. And in a consumer-driven society, a lot of people and companies are trying to get our worship. Pay attention. Your character should not be for sale. Stand in your belief in what is right and what is wrong. Regardless of the circumstance, how you feel in your soul is what matters, and your soul was given to you by God.

CHAPTER 11

THE WORK

You're probably looking at all of this saying, "Wow, John, that's a lot of work to do!" The answer is, "Yeah, it is!" We only get one life, and our lives are a gift. Regardless of how it starts, at some point, we get to make the choices that dictate our future. We have work to do, and the good news is that we can do the work! We can show up every day with passion and purpose, a crusade and a cause, an enemy to take on, and the ability to go after it. We can be the men our wives and our children dream us to be, the men they pray for us to be.

Is it going to be easy? Nope! But you know what? Nothing easy is worth it.

There's a great scene in the movie *A League Of Their Own*, in which Tom Hanks plays an older, experienced, washed-up baseball-player-turned-women's-baseball-coach named Jimmy Dugan. Where he once resisted and hated his job, he ends up falling in love with both it and his players. Naturally, they go on to do great things but his star player is leaving in the middle of the season, right before the world championship series. Like any good coach, he confronts her, and she gives him a poor excuse as to why she's giving up. After really digging in, he finally gets her to reveal the true issue. "It just got too hard," she says. His response is a line that lives (in my humble opinion) in cinematic history: "It's supposed to be hard. If it wasn't hard, everyone would do it. It's the hard that makes it great!"

It's the hard that makes it great. That is my challenge to you, mighty warrior: embrace the hard.

In the summer of 2005, I faced an extremely hard challenge, one I didn't see coming. My response to it set in motion the makings of the life we live today. Shortly after Trish and I moved to Florida, I started a business. I was so attracted to the crusade of the company that I fully jumped in. Trish and I were very good at being employees, but we had no experience when it came to going into business. Through sheer grit and determination, we learned the business. While she stayed home, I worked construction by day and the business at night. Our goals to keep her home, keep the kids out of daycare, and make a significant income drove us on; however, it challenged our comfort zone in many ways.

Looking back on it now, I see that God was using this experience to transform us, and in the summer of 2005, in the middle of the company's International Convention, I had a moment. I'll never forget it. In an instant, I saw our future lives, and I saw what was possible for our children. I saw the people they could be and the opportunities that were ahead of them. I saw how radically different their lives could be if we could just continue to persevere through the obstacles in front of us. The challenge, however, was that our marriage was feeling the brunt of those obstacles. I knew fear was wreaking havoc on our family, and if we continued to let it reign, it would either pull us apart or destroy our business, and therefore our possible future. In that moment, I had a "Man Up!" moment. On the floor of this huge stadium, in the middle of about 60,000 people, I stood my ground and said, "Trish, I will no longer let fear rule our household. If you choose not to follow me in this, I don't know what to tell you, but our family is too important to let this go, and this is where we are going." I'm sure Trish has a completely different version of that story, but that's the way I remember it. We had a heated discussion later regarding it, but that moment was when I chose to dig in and fight for her and our children. It was a defining moment in our lives, just like me telling my mom I wanted to live with my father. Why do I say it was a "Man Up!" moment? Because up to that point, I never stood up and led like that. I never rose up and took a stand for her, in what initially appeared to be in defiance of her. I share this story with you because it was one of those moments where I learned how much my wife needed me to be the leader, warrior, and champion for our family. There comes a time in our lives where all the experiences, pain, and suffering lead up to the *moment*—the moment when you're anointed and you step into your destiny.

In the Old Testament, in the book of Judges, there is the story of Gideon. When we come to his part in the larger Biblical story, Gideon is going about his chores, threshing wheat, but he's doing it in secret because he's hiding it from the Midianites, who were harassing Israel during this time. An Angel of God appears to him and says: *"The Lord is with you, you mighty man of valor!"*

Notice that the angel calls him a "mighty man" while he's still doing his chores! This means that God spoke to Gideon as He knew him to be, not by what he had done up to that point in his life.

Gideon then asks the angel, *"My Lord, if the Lord is with us, why then has all this happened to us? And where are all His miracles which our fathers told us about....?"*

The angel, which is God, tells him that he has been chosen to save Israel from the Midianites. Gideon's response is one I think most men are asking daily: "Who am I that you would choose me?"

The answer to that question has been the same throughout history, but we keep thinking it's someone else's. It's not! It's you! YOU are the "mighty warrior." You are the one chosen to deliver your "nation." That nation starts with you, then moves on to your wife, your children, and so on.

I want you to grasp something—an extremely profound idea that, when comprehended, has the power to alter your life in an amazing way. In this incredibly vast universe, there is only one you. Now, don't go and dismiss that as a trivial fact. Never before, and certainly not after, has there ever been *you*. You have been placed here, on this planet, during this time in history. That's not random, and it certainly isn't an accident. I truly believe there is a reason and a purpose to each of our lives, and when you discover what that is, that's when I believe we move from existing to living.

You were not created to exist in your life. You are supposed to live; truly live with full expression. I say that a lot—"full expression." What does that mean? It's the Four Pillars in action. It involves being authentic, and saying what needs to be said. It's expressing yourself, and doing so from a position of humility, so that those around you know that you are here to love them, serve them, grow amazing relationships with them, and impact others around you. "Full expression" means displaying character through integrity and morality; to stand firm in what you say and to display a clear distinction of right and wrong. It's about giving permission to all of the people around you to live fully expressed as well.

I love the fact that throughout the Bible, God continues to call those who were not yet living in the destiny He created them for. Why? Because it's continuous proof that we can become more when we stop listening to the lies of The Enemy, stop drifting in our reality, unplug from "The Matrix," and start listening to the Creator of All constantly telling us who we are, why He created us, and the purpose and plans He has for our lives.

The truly great and historical people we speak about today didn't intentionally set out to be that. For most, their moment showed up and they stepped into it. I believe without a shadow of doubt that our moments constantly show up, just waiting for us to step into them. Greatness isn't achieved in one moment. It's a thousand different decisions leading up to one big one;

but how can that moment come to fruition if we don't move forward in strength when those decisions show up?

I referenced King Saul earlier, in the chapter on integrity. Do you want to know why Saul was stripped of the kingdom, even though God chose him to lead? It was because he could not accept the fact that he was the one chosen. There are two verses in scripture that illustrate this. The first is in 1 Samuel 9:21: *"And Saul answered and said, 'Am I not a Benjamite, of the smallest of the tribes of Israel, and my family the least of all the families of the tribe of Benjamin? Why then do you speak like this to me?'"*

Saul is responding to the prophet Samuel, who has let him know that he's been chosen by God to be king. I think most of us would probably have a similar response, yet Saul couldn't accept it. A short time later, when it's time to reveal Saul to the people, here is what the Bible says about where he is when the people cannot locate him: *"And the Lord answered, "There he is, hidden among the baggage." (1 Samuel 10:22)*

"Hidden among the baggage!" Hidden

among his issues. Hidden among his belief. Hidden among his past. Hidden among his doubt. Saul couldn't get pass his own belief system. And so, I challenge you, mighty warrior: get past your issues! Stop hiding amongst your baggage.

What's also interesting is David's response when he is called. We all know the story of David and Goliath. We tell it to our children, and it's referenced throughout history. David faces the giant in his life and says: *"Who is this uncircumcised Philistine, that he should defy the armies of the living God?" "The Lord, who delivered me from the paw of the lion and from the paw of the bear, He will deliver me from the hand of this Philistine." (1 Samuel 17:26)*

What I didn't share with you is that, just like Saul, Samuel let David know that he was going to be king. Both men were anointed, yet one couldn't believe it and the other embraced it fully.

What about you? What have you been called to, anointed in, and yet keep putting off? I doubt a prophet is going to come and anoint your head with oil, but I do believe God has anointed your heart. Will you run toward your destiny the way David ran towards Goliath, or will you continue to hide among your baggage? I challenge you: BE more, DO more, and ultimately, HAVE more!

Remember, "It's the hard that makes it great." It's not going to be easy. It will be a battle, and you can do it.

CHAPTER 12

THE POWER OF YOUR POSSE

"You are the average of the five people you spend your time with."—Jim Rhon

I truly thought this book was done, but then I realized that if I don't put a chapter in here discussing the power of your posse—your circle, the people you spend the bulk of your time with—and the power of those associations, then all the things covered in this book might not happen because of self-sabotage. Your circle matters!

Who we spend our time with has so much influence on who we are and how we show up in our lives. It's our level of awareness that dictates who we surround ourselves with, so we need to have a brief discussion regarding it and what it actually means.

Our awareness is how we perceive the world around us. Let's say two people are sitting outside a Starbucks, having coffee, when all of a sudden there's an explosion in the parking lot. The explosion is what has happened. Each person's perception of what has happened, however, will be different. Why? Because we all perceive our reality in our own unique way, and that has everything to do with our level of awareness.

Before Donald Trump was President Trump, he was a businessman. During his career, he lost and remade billions of dollars. How is that possible when another person can lose $100,000 dollars and never make it back? Because President Trump's mindset and level of awareness is operating on a higher plane, at a higher level. And because of this, he sees the world differently than someone else. He's able to process things differently and therefore react differently.

Thoughts are proven to be energy, and energy always seeks its equal vibration. Therefore, what we think about attracts the things that are vibrating at that same frequency. The most common example of this is when you buy a new car, or are thinking of one. You may never have seen a certain model out there before, but now? It's like they are everywhere! Recently, I've been toying with the idea of getting a Jeep. Before I started to think about this and research them, I never really paid much attention to any Jeep around me. They just weren't in my reality. But now, I see them everywhere! Why? Because my brain is going to filter out the things that are either aiding in my survival or my goals. A Jeep just wasn't in either category. That's the power of thought.

Now think about your associations, your relationships. Look at the level of thought that the people you associate with most have. What are they thinking about? What are they talking about? Are they talking about good things or bad things? Are they positive or negative? Are they gossiping or are they seeking to learn more? Are they praising and blessing, or are they condescending or condemning? Our relationships are very, very important, and our circle, the people around us, have a direct effect on us. We are simply the average level of their collective thought level. It is, therefore, really important to pay attention to who's in your circle.

There are so many great examples of the "power of the posse" throughout history. We study them, we examine them, and we celebrate them. So many of them have gone on to do incredible things that have grown our country.

A great Biblical example is again in the story of King David.

David, by now, has been king for some time, and has made some serious mistakes. His own son Absalom, having plotted against him, wants the throne, and chases David and his men out of the kingdom and into the wilderness. Eventually, those loyal to David meet Absalom's army on the field of battle. Never losing love for his son, David directs his commander Joab to *"Deal gently for my sake with the young man Absalom."* Joab, greatly insulated by Absalom's rebellion, sees an opportunity to take out Absalom and strikes him through the heart, killing him. Overcome with grief, David locks himself away, hiding himself from his men and the people most loyal to him. What follows next is a powerful example of having the right people in your circle.

"Joab was told, "The king is weeping and

mourning for Absalom." And for the whole army the victory that day was turned into mourning, because on that day the troops heard it said, "The king is grieving for his son." The men stole into the city that day as men who are ashamed when they flee from battle. The king covered his face and cried aloud, "O my son Absalom! O Absalom, my son, my son!" Then Joab went into the house to the king and said, "Today you have humiliated all your men, who have just saved your life and the lives of your sons and daughters and the lives of your wives and concubines. You love those who hate you and hate those who love you. You have made it clear today that the commanders and their men mean nothing to you. I see that you would be pleased if Absalom were alive today and all of us were dead. Now go out and encourage your men. I swear by the Lord that if you don't go out, not a man will be left with you by nightfall. This will be worse for you than all the calamities that have come on you from your youth till now."

Whenever I read this story, I'm amazed by the strength of Joab, and his willingness to say and do what was necessary to protect his friend. David needed somebody who understood him as a man, accepted him for who he was, and yet was man enough himself to tell him what was most important. David, in Joab, had a man in his inner circle who lived in integrity, authenticity, humility, and morality. Joab had to do what he knew he needed to do. He had to do the right thing, and he had to be transparent. He knew right from wrong, and he stepped up to David and said, "If you don't fix this, you're going to lose everything." Joab was an important part of David's circle. So, again, I ask you: who's in your circle?

Back while I was still a teacher, I struck up a friendship with my dentist. As we hung out more and more, I began to see that he thought on a level far greater than my own level of thought. He processed his daily reality far differently than I did. My problems and challenges were so much smaller than his. I understood as we got to know each other that I was going to have to change. There were things he knew and things he had learned along the way that I did not. I knew I had to level up.

Let's do a little exercise. Who are the five closest people to you right now? Rate each person through the four pillars: integrity,

humility, authenticity, and morality, on a scale
of one to five.

Integrity	Integrity	Integrity	Integrity	Integrity
1 2 3 4 5	1 2 3 4 5	1 2 3 4 5	1 2 3 4 5	1 2 3 4 5
Humility	Humility	Humility	Humility	Humility
1 2 3 4 5	1 2 3 4 5	1 2 3 4 5	1 2 3 4 5	1 2 3 4 5
Authenticity	Authenticity	Authenticity	Authenticity	Authenticity
1 2 3 4 5	1 2 3 4 5	1 2 3 4 5	1 2 3 4 5	1 2 3 4 5
Morality	Morality	Morality	Morality	Morality
1 2 3 4 5	1 2 3 4 5	1 2 3 4 5	1 2 3 4 5	1 2 3 4 5

The goal of this exercise is to get your inner
circle filled with people that score highly in each
category. Remember, it starts with intention.
You have to *be* a person who scores high in each
category, so you can *do* what a person like that
does, then *have* those around you that resonate
at the same energy frequency. How would life
be different if you leveled up your associations?
I can only share with you from personal
experience that my life is much richer, deeper,

and filled with more passion and joy because of it.

If you want your circle of people around you to grow, then it starts on the inside through personal development: reading books, listening to podcasts and audio books, and attending seminars. Did I do any of these things before realizing that I needed to level up? Nope! I joke that I used to read Stephen King and *Star Wars* books, and magazines like *Modern Drummer, PC Gamer*, and *Sports Illustrated* (at least one time a year). There's nothing wrong with any of those things, but if I wanted to grow my influence, business, income, and influence on my family, church, and the circle around me, then I had to first start on the inside. I had to get better. We move from the inside to the outside, not the other way around.

When we change on the inside, we raise our level of thought and kick off a higher vibration. That vibration will then start to attract people who think the same way. You will soon start to notice how you hear and say things differently. You will start having conversations with new people who are attracted to your level of thought, thereby increasing your circle. Eventually, a Mastermind Group may develop.

Mastermind Groups are people that you associate with where the level of thought is collective. Everybody's thinking the same way and creating incredible things together. David had his Mighty Men. King Arthur had his Knights of the Round Table. Franklin Roosevelt had the Brain Trust. Andrew Carnegie had the Steel Mill. Henry Ford had The Vagabonds. Jesus had the Twelve Disciples.

Your posse, like everything in your life, is intentional. Life isn't something that just happens. It's created through intent. Pay attention to who you surround yourself with, because your future depends on it! This is no joke. This is your great destiny. It's your life. God created you for a reason and a purpose. You can do it, and the next best version of you is right around the corner!

Feel free to reach out to me. You can find me on most social media platforms at "@JPuritz" or "John C. Puritz." Let me know how I can support you.

You have what it takes.

You can be the man you were created to be, so please, for yourself, your family, your community, and the world—*Man Up, Already!*

RESOURCES

WEBSITES USED FOR RESEARCH

Pornography

https://www.webroot.com/us/en/resources/tips-articles/internet-pornography-by-the-numbers

Singe Parenting

https://www.verywellfamily.com/single-parent-census-data-2997668

Divorce

https://www.wf-lawyers.com/divorce-statistics-and-facts/

Gun Violence

https://www.usatoday.com/story/news/2017/10/10/men-special-risk-guns-they-love/734961001/

Drug Abuse

https://www.drugabuse.gov/publications/research-reports/substance-use-in-women/sex-gender-differences-in-substance-use

MOTION PICTURES CITED

A League of their Own, Dir. Penny Marshall, Per. Tom Hanks, Columbia Pictures, 1992

Rocky Balboa, Dir. Sylvester Stallone, Perf. Sylvester Stallone, MGM, 2006

BOOKS CITED

John Eldredge, *Wild at Heart,* Thomas Nelson, 2001

Wallace D. Wattles, *The Science of Getting Rich,* Best Success Books 2017, Originally published in 1910

Napoleon Hill, *Think and Grow Rich,* Penguin Group, 2003, Originally published in 1913

SONGS CITED

Sanctus Real, *"Lead Me,"* Sparrow Records, 2010

Made in the USA
Columbia, SC
08 May 2019